THE MALPRACTICE OF PSYCHIATRISTS

Publication Number 874

AMERICAN LECTURE SERIES®

A Monograph in

The BANNERSTONE DIVISION *of*
AMERICAN LECTURES IN BEHAVIORAL SCIENCE AND LAW

Edited by

RALPH SLOVENKO, B.E., LL.B., M.A., Ph.D.

Wayne State University
Law School
Detroit, Michigan

THE MALPRACTICE OF PSYCHIATRISTS

Malpractice in Psychoanalysis, Psychotherapy and Psychiatry

By

DONALD J. DAWIDOFF

Attorney-at-Law
New York, New York

CHARLES C THOMAS · PUBLISHER

Springfield · Illinois · U.S.A.

Published and Distributed Throughout the World by
CHARLES C THOMAS • PUBLISHER
BANNERSTONE HOUSE
301-327 East Lawrence Avenue, Springfield, Illinois, U.S.A.

ISBN 0-398-02711-0
Library of Congress Catalog Card Number: 72-88462

Printed in the United States of America
HH-11

To
NICKY and SALLY

Foreword

The rapid increase following World War II in the rate of medical malpractice suits has corresponded with the changing patterns of medical practice and physician status. The patient no longer believes, as he once did, that the physician can do no wrong. Once a relative rarity, malpractice suits are now common throughout the United States. According to the American Medical Association, one-fourth of all physicians in the country will be sued for malpractice before the end of their careers. Those most likely affected are the anesthesiologist, orthopedist, surgeon and obstetrician. The rapport between them and their patients tends to be thin, and their errors tend to be self-evident. At the other end of the spectrum is the psychiatrist.

The psychiatrist is the "talking doctor," as contrasted to the surgeon, the "cutting doctor." Almost anything seems acceptable in "talking." Most of the litigation involving psychiatrists has resulted from physical and not psychic damage to the patient. The relatively few cases against psychiatrists have been based on faulty diagnosis, improper certification in commitment proceedings, failure to exercise adequate suicide precautions, breach of confidentiality, drug treatment that may have caused brain damage or other adverse physical damage, and improper administration of medication or electric shock treatment. There are also a few criminal and civil cases involving psychiatrists who have had sexual relations with their patients.

However, there do not appear to be any cases involving improper or defective psychotherapeutic or analytic technique. Contributing to the few malpractice suits against psychiatrists is the fact that no one wants his personal life revealed in a courtroom. And an allegation of breach of contract is difficult to sustain, for at the beginning of treatment, a point is made to the patient of promising nothing.

Insurance company statistics estimate that the number of

psychiatric malpractice cases is relatively small, amounting to approximately 1.5 claims per 100 psychiatrists per year, far less than the estimated medical malpractice rate of one claim per four practitioners per year. However, most insurance carriers have placed psychiatry in the "risk-rating category" containing general practitioners, even though the loss ratio of psychiatrists is not as high as that of general practitioners.

The literature, both legal and psychiatric, on psychiatric malpractice consists of only a few articles and deals mainly with the areas of patient suicide, shock therapy and involuntary commitment. Donald J. Dawidoff was the author of one of the seminal articles, and he has now developed the subject in this comprehensive book.

In this work, Dawidoff argues that there can be a cause of action by a patient against his psychiatrist not only for malpractice in improperly rendering electroshock and insulin shock therapy or drug therapy and for wrongful commitment or negligently allowing suicide but also for the faulty or negligent rendering of psychoanalysis and psychotherapy. The argument is based upon the conformity to the conventional medical malpractice standard of the forms of verbal therapy.

The difficulty of formulating the standard of care is described, and the medical model of the standard of care which must be breached for a cause of action to accrue is set forth. Verbal negligence occurs for violation of the duty to speak skillfully and carefully. Possible negligence occurs in the misapplication of transference and countertransference.

Next there are discussions of problems of proof, proximate cause and the method of proving a variety of injuries, including emotional distress. Guideposts for the psychiatrist are discussed together with consent. Problems of sexual abuse of the transference are described and the whole range of encounter group physical touching evaluated against a malpractice standard. The drug abuse cases are considered and some definition of the guidelines for legally protected psychiatric care undertaken.

The book discusses hospitalization, and an argument is made against the doctrine of judicial privilege to protect physician testimony in commitment hearings. Suicide and administration of shock therapy are also examined, and lastly some critical comments on the role of the courts are set forth.

Throughout there is a use of case as well as text material in an attempt to illuminate legal doctrine by psychiatric literature. Special emphasis is given to the English case of *Landau v. Werner,* for it stands as the crucial though not uncriticized precedent for psychiatric malpractice in the verbal therapies.

Donald J. Dawidoff, born in 1934 in New York City, grew up in Manhasset, New York, and attended Manhasset High School where he was valedictorian of his class. At Harvard College, from which he graduated *cum laude* in 1957, he was on the dean's list and majored in American history and literature. He attended the Yale Law School where he was a member of the Barristers' Union, receiving his LL.B. in 1962.

Thereafter he practiced law in Washington, D.C., and New York City and served with the Office of the General Counsel of the United States Department of Health, Education and Welfare and as a Trial Attorney with the United States Securities and Exchange Commission. He has taught at the George Washington University Graduate School of Public Law and is the author of articles in legal periodicals. He is a member of the New York and District of Columbia Bars. He presently practices law in New York City.

RALPH SLOVENKO
Editor, American Lecture Series in Behavioral Science and Law

Introduction

While a great deal has been written about the interaction of law and psychiatry,[1] malpractice by psychiatrists, and especially malpractice in psychoanalysis and psychotherapy has been a neglected byway.[2] Its omission is important, for it is suggested that the volume of cases in law offices and the courts far outdistances the number of appellate court decisions.

It will be the attempt here to describe malpractice by psychiatrists and especially to examine the nature of, and remedy for, malpractice in the verbal therapies of psychoanalysis and psychotherapy. This involves discussion of the nature of psychotherapeutic care and the tenets of malpractice. The difficulties awaiting application of the canons of malpractice to such therapy are explored at length. Furthermore, the specialized legal theories of breach of fiduciary duty, undue influence and words negligently spoken are applied to psychotherapy and psychoanalysis, and throughout, a sampling of the psychiatric literature is set forth to indicate the doctrinal recognition of concepts described.

Finally, other psychiatric therapies such as shock treatment and hospitalization are examined in order to broaden and provide comparison with the discussion of verbal therapy.

Throughout the book, it is not only the case material that is

1 *See, e.g.* Katz, Goldstein and Dershowitz: *Psychoanalysis, Psychiatry and Law* (1967); Davidson: *Forensic Psychiatry* (2nd ed., 1965); Watson: *Psychiatry for Lawyers* (1968).

2 The initial work of two psychiatrists is fundamental. *See* Bellamy: "Malpractice Risks Confronting the Psychiatrist: A Nationwide Fifteen-year Study of Appellate Court Cases, 1946 to 1961," 118 *Am. J. Psychiat.* 709 (1962); Bellamy: "Malpractice in Psychiatry," *In A Symposium on the Medico-Legal Aspects of Private Psychiatric Practice,* 25 (1965); Davidson, *op. cit. supra,* note 1, chapter 16.

Morse, in "The Tort Liability of the Psychiatrist," 19 *Baylor L. Rev.* 208 (1967) and this author, in "The Malpractice of Psychiatrists," 1966 *Duke L. J.* 696, have added to the literature, while Louisell and Williams: *Trial of Medical Malpractice Cases* (1970) collect and add brief general insight to the cases. *See* also Annot. 99 *A.L.R.2d* 599 (1965).

relied upon but, by necessity, application of analogous doctrine and psychiatric writing. Some of the questions examined are: Can there be legal malpractice in psychoanalysis and psychotherapy? How may these techniques be described? What are the characteristics and legal consequences of verbal therapy? What is the doctrine of words negligently spoken? In what manner does fiduciary obligation attach to the psychiatrist? What of the patient's obligations? How does consent apply? What are the methods of guarding against wrongful commitment to a mental hospital? How is suicide regulated? How does malpractice effect the rendering of shock therapies? What must be proven to establish a case in psychiatric malpractice? What are the guideposts for the practicing psychiatrist who seeks to avoid liability for malpractice?

Acknowledgments

Portions of this book are reprinted from the Duke Law Journal, Copyright 1966 by the *Duke Law Journal* and are reprinted by permission of the copyright holder. Original citation: 1966 *Duke Law Journal* 696. Copies of the issue containing the article may be obtained from the Managing Editor, *Duke Law Journal,* Duke University School of Law, Durham, North Carolina 27706.

Selections reprinted from INSIGHT AND RESPONSIBILITY by Erik H. Erikson by permission of W. W. Norton & Company, Inc. Copyright © 1964 by Erik H. Erikson.

I wish to acknowledge the many helpful comments of my friends and associates in writing this book. My special gratitude goes to Paul S. Weisberg, M.D. for his invaluable assistance in the original formulation of this work.

CONTENTS

THE MALPRACTICE OF PSYCHIATRISTS

Chapter I

Can There Be Malpractice In Psychoanalysis And Psychotherapy?

The primary question for consideration at the outset is whether or not psychotherapy and psychoanalysis in their diagnostic and treating phases fall within the scope of the legal remedy of malpractice. Stated another way, can a patient who can prove that her psychiatrist was unskilled, careless or disloyal[1] in treating her by psychotherapy or psychoanalysis be awarded damages for the injury or harm she suffers? We must begin by examining the character of psychiatric diagnoses and treatments and then turn to the legal requisites for an action in malpractice. One word of hesitation. It is not necessarily true that because psychiatry is not exactly the prototype of medical science or art that it may not be examined by conventional malpractice techniques. It may be, for example, that the rest of medical science is not itself completely unitary. Some types of medical mistakes, for example, are granted the case-saving remedy of *res ipsa loquitur.* Some failures in psychiatric treatment have already been granted recourse to this type of remedial aid. Those that have been denied it seem to have been correctly treated. But malpractice in itself may not be a totally monolithic form of action. It stretches and yields to advances in the healing arts and may have elasticity enough for psychiatry's innovations. Similarly, there may be other forms of action which can absorb psychotherapeutic carelessness and disloyalty. And finally, it may be that new forms of remedy may be thought through to stand at the side of the harmfulness

[1] *Cf.* Freud: *An Outline of Psycho-Analysis* 32 (1940) (Strachey, ed. 1969): "However much the analyst may be tempted to become a teacher, model and ideal for other people and to create men in his own image, he should not forget that that is not his task in the analytic relationship, and indeed he will be disloyal to his task if he allows himself to be led by his own inclinations."

inherent in these, as in other new forms of human endeavor. But first we must look at malpractice, because it is the classic form of remedy for medical misfeasance.

THE MEDICAL SETTING

Psychiatry is that branch of medicine which deals with the care and treatment of mental illness. While it has been suggested that the very concept of mental illness is a misnomer,[2] we shall assume for the present purposes that the concept is a valid one. We shall also consider the psychiatrist as a medical doctor trained as a physician. Thus, we shall discuss the non-physician's practicing psychoanalysis, psychiatry and sensitivity training only as they become liable to clients while practicing their art. The lack of a Doctor of Medicine degree may in different cases create an exemption from the kinds of legal remedies herein discussed, though perhaps not from other ones. Thus, for example, the non-psychiatrist might well be liable for a breach of his contract with a client or for negligence not amounting to psychiatric malpractice.

Psychiatry itself may be defined as the care and treatment of mental disease or illness by the canons of medical care. The psychiatrist or the non-psychiatrist may both practice psychoanalysis, while only the psychiatrist may prescribe drugs or engage in chemotherapy. The basic shock therapies may also only be employed in treatment by the medically trained psychiatrist, though it may be administered by psychiatrist and non-psychiatrist alike. By contrast, the non-psychiatrist physician may utilize and prescribe any and all of the treatments employed by psychiatrists, though it may be arguable that the use of such modalities as psychoanalysis by a physician or person not trained in them may constitute a tort. This may extend to the use of encounter group techniques or even to conventional group therapy by the psychiatrist not specifically trained in these methods. In this manner, he may become liable in tort. On the other hand, it is likewise maintainable that in an area of medicine where innovation is widespread and the fixed pattern of treatment relatively uncertain,

2 Szasz: *The Myth of Mental Illness* 4 (1961); *but see* Stafford-Clark, Book Review, 74 *Yale L.J.* 392 (1964).

i.e. the treatment called for in any instance, it is in the interest of any given patient and psychiatry in general to allow *experiment* and innovation with the psychiatrist applying techniques about which he knows relatively little and which he has seldom, if ever, used.[3]

We shall deal here with treatment modes used by those ministering to the mentally ill. We may thus consider confinement to mental or general hospitals; electroshock and insulin shock; chemotherapy; psychoanalysis; psychotherapy, individually or in groups; and encounter techniques.

We may include in confinement to a mental or other hospital the various means by which ill persons are placed in mental or other hospitals for care and treatment. We do not mean to limit this to their involuntary detention, as has for some purposes been advanced. We shall discuss instead all the means, both compulsory and non-compulsory, by which persons are placed in hospital or sanitarium-style institutions. This might also include residential facilities or so-called "halfway houses" where persons pass therapeutic time away from their own homes.

Typically, these facilities used to be "closed-door" places where locks bolted the sleeping, eating, and recreational areas of institutions. Now, however, it may be more common for some patients to be given the run of the grounds of such places and to have the option, under some forms of hospitalization, to end their confinement either for some hours, days or altogether.

Dependent upon the type of confinement, psychiatrists may be seen to perform widely differing tasks. Thus, they may act as expert witnesses for a judicial proceeding in which, alone or in conjunction with a statutorily prescribed companion number of psychiatrists or physicians, they may examine a person and make their clinical judgment that the person is mentally ill or perhaps a danger to himself or others. In judicial proceedings, the judge himself may make the determination that hospitalization is necessary. In non-judicial but public proceedings, a physician may directly achieve the confinement on his own determina-

[3] Nevertheless, it is generally stated that departure from "generally accepted methods" is at the doctor's own risk. *See* Davidson: *Forensic Psychiatry* 289 (2d ed., 1965).

tion that it is necessary. In private confinement, there may be no judgment as to the patient's likelihood of being a danger to himself or others but merely a confinement thought to be in the best interests of his health or person. The more private the act, the more likely that malpractice or some other legal remedy will avail.

There are also differences as to the nature of the confinement. In some cases, it is merely to place the patient in a restful, dependent environment where he may, by baths and rest, resume a vigor that he has temporarily lost. At the other extreme, such hospitalization may mean months of confinement to a complete treatment facility where his every act is prescribed by a therapeutic, vocational, rehabilitative and recreational environment. The latter may involve a whole treatment team which operates under the institution's resident psychiatric staff. Thus nurses, occupational therapists, custodial persons, psychologists, resident psychiatrists—anyone who has direct personal contact or judgment over a sick person—may all contribute to a treatment process under the conjoint leadership of the outside committing psychiatrist and his institutional counterparts. In between these extremes may be a wealth of psychiatric hospitals where the private psychiatrist meets his patient, including the patient in his outside treatment groups. At the same time, the hospital staff also attempts to treat the patient by chemotherapy prescribed by the outside psychiatrist as well as by including him in the hospital's therapy groups. Some hospitals have a highly developed sense of community in which they try to include the patient, requiring him to participate in "town meetings" where the problems of living together as a "therapeutic community" are discussed and resolved. Let it not be thought that the psychiatrist who participated in the hospitalization of the patient (for the patient may have signed himself in using a signature that also waived, or attempted to waive, his rights against the hospital) has no liability here, for as we shall see, he may have a continuing legal responsibility for the acts of others as well as those of himself for injuries that take place in the hospital.

The drugs that physicians prescribe for a patient in or out of a hospital range from hallucinogenic and adrenalin-style drugs to those which are prescribed for the limitation of anxiety or which attempt to deal with depression. Such drugs may be dangerous without certain restraints or for persons with different blood or certain kinds of symptoms or chemical makeup. There is a wide literature on the results of certain dosages and accompanying drugs and the prescribing physician may be charged with a certain knowledge of such indications. Linked with the prescribing physician is the pharmacist who sells the drug and most emphatically the nurse who may administer the drug. The physician's responsibility begins rather than ends with the writing of the prescription. He must know his patient—just as the stockbroker under N.A.S.D. and Stock Exchange rule must know his customer—and he may be negligent if he gives the right pill to the wrong patient. At this point, as we shall see later, the patient may himself have duties, such as following the prescribed dosage, which he cannot overlook when seeking to fix liability for injury upon his psychiatrist. The acts of the patient might raise issues of contributory negligence. Some of the patient's acts might operate as a bar to an action against the psychiatrist, while others, theoretically at least, might create an action against the patient on the part of the psychiatrist himself, such as where his reputation is injured.

Some drugs, of course, are administered by injection, especially with large doses meant for the very sick. One of the drugs that has classically been administered to mentally ill persons is insulin. It was intended to induce a shock to the system of the patient so that he might be relieved of mood disturbance or depression. Similar treatment has been undertaken with an electrically, rather than a chemically, induced shock. Both insulin and electroshock therapies require care in administration as well as in prescription, and both have certain dangerous side effects that have been clinically noted.

PSYCHOANALYSIS AND PSYCHOTHERAPY

But the major focus of much treatment has been and is now psychoanalysis and psychotherapy. Psychoanalysis is a treatment whereby cure is sought by talks between the physician or the therapist and one or a group of patients. During this treatment, the patient sits or reclines in the presence of the therapist and speaks of his past, present and future life and seeks, through the guidance of the therapist, to think, talk and live through various aspects of his life in order to more fully understand his own conscious and unconscious thought and action processes. He is guided by interpretation of his spoken words and his acts both in and out of the presence of his physician to understand the dynamics of his personality and thereby to change his behavior and to live in comfort or relative comfort with his own inner experiences and thought processes. Classically, he works through his feelings about those closest to him in his past and present and learns to resolve his infantile neurosis, or as Freud has stated it:

> We serve the patient in various functions as an authority and a substitute for his parents, as a teacher and educator and we have done the best for him if, as analysts, we raise the mental processes in his ego to a normal level, transform what has become unconscious and repressed into preconscious material and thus return it once more to the possession of his ego.[4]

In order to accomplish this aim, he unconsciously attributes to the psychiatrist or analyst those feelings which he may have repressed towards his own parents. This attribution process is called the transference, and it is through the creation, experiencing and resolution of these feelings that he becomes well. This process may be coincident with an identification with the therapist whereby the patient learns to think, style and model himself after the therapist.[5] The therapist himself, in the meantime, develops a set of feelings and reactions towards the patient. This process, called the countertransference, consists of the therapist's own anxiety and other reaction to the deeply personal experience of the patient. Psychotherapy has psychoanalysis as its root but may include more intervention by the therapist.

In many cases, a so-called group therapy may replace the individual therapy. In such cases, groups of persons ranging from two to perhaps ten or fifteen persons sit together with the therapist or therapists and talk through their feelings and actions with active comment upon each other's spoken words and behavior. The rule of such groups is openness and honesty about even the

[4] Freud: *An Outline of Psycho-Analysis* 38 (Strachey, ed. 1969).
[5] *Id.* at 32.

most potentially shameful aspects of their thoughts and activities or about those reactions to other group members or therapists that might not be appropriate in normal social discourse. In the more radical treatments, physical touching,[6] pushing, embracing and even perhaps sexual intercourse[7] occur, with the aim of honesty, openness and responsiveness paramount.

This is where the so-called encounter movement has made its contribution. The encounter groups or sensitivity training workshops as they are often called, join physician, psychologist or lay leader together in sessions of talking, exercise, psychodrama or other touching and physical activities all designed to change behavior from balked self-deception to more spontaneous, honest and ego-consistent thought patterns and systems of action. These groups, formed outside of the psychiatric field, have recently made large and definite contributions to psychotherapy and have begun to make permissible what was often thought anathema to psychiatrist-patient interaction.[8]

There are only certain things which separate psychoanalytic psychiatry from its specialized brethren. In the first place, the medium of practice may be only spoken words. There is a large expanse of practice which makes use of drugs, yet the physical administration of chemical matter is not essentially distinguishable from the other circumstances in which drugs are administered to nonpsychiatric patients. The use of words, however, harks back to the general practitioner with soothing advice and bedside manner. This, however, is not the only role for words coming from a psychiatrist to the patient.

In the first place, we may start with therapy which is closest to the act of the general practitioner just spoken of. This is so-called supportive therapy, where no real attempt is made to probe and analyze the patient's behavior, but instead the whole weight of the physician's words is directed towards comforting

6 *See* Schutz: *Joy* (1967); Howard: *Please Touch* (1970); Ruitenbeek: *The New Group Therapies* 127 (1970).

7 Shepard: *The Love Treatment* (1971).

8 *See, e.g.,* Freud, *op. cit. supra,* p. 33: "Real sexual relations between patients and analysts are out of the question, and even the subtler methods of satisfaction, such as the giving of preference, intimacy and so on, are only sparingly granted by the analyst."

and easing and providing a bastion for the patient against outside pressures and intrapsychic conflict. In such situations, the psychiatrist may offer soothing words and comforting modes of thought for the patient.

One distinct difficulty that may arise in the use of this mode of therapy has to do with its choice. It may be that the psychiatrist's choice of this therapeutic mode has to do with a mistaken impression on his part that the patient cannot be changed or moved to new and more healthy patterns of behavior. It may be, instead, that the doctor analyzes the patient as too embedded in a particular behavior pattern, such as schizophrenia, for example, to be able to take on more active and healthy patterns of living. Such a choice may then be grounds for an allegation of malpractice, given that the requisite standards are not met. Thus, perhaps, administration of supportive therapy may deprive the patient of the analytically oriented therapy which could move him out of a depression. The error here might then be charged to faulty diagnosis on the part of the psychiatrist, difficult though it may be to ascribe damage to the use of a therapy that was never, in fact, administered. Like the damages for a corporate opportunity that was never, in fact, enjoyed by the corporation, it is difficult here to find damages for a therapy which was never administered.

Aside from supportive or maintenance therapy, there is the large field of analytically oriented ameliorative therapy. In such therapy, the attempt is to identify with words the behavior pattern which the patient is undergoing and by this process of analysis to give the patient governing command of the symptom in his behavior and thus enable him to triumph over it by his own control. It is the mode of this therapy to impart insight to the patient so that he can objectify and control the damaging symptoms in his behavior pattern. The analytically oriented therapy is imparted verbally in an individual or group setting, with the patient lying on a couch in the classical analysis or sitting in a chair in psychotherapy as distinguished from psychoanalysis. In these therapies, and in analysis, the patient learns through seeing and feeling his behavior pattern in a setting removed from the actual figures in his life who have called forth his harmful emotional responses. He may impute to the therapist or analyst the role of an oppressive parent and learn through seeing himself react to this neutral figure to abandon his damaging feelings toward the parent. This psychiatric imputation is called the transference. Thus he may feel tied to a parent and the latter's judgment of his acts so that he has become dependent upon that parent for the queues and signals of his own behavior. In the therapy, he may learn to follow his own rather than someone else's pattern of living. For the therapist's task or that of the analyst would be to give the patient once again the intellectual and emotional experience of the unhealthy child-parent relationship and to point out and allow the patient to realize the faultiness of the behavior pattern, or at least its consequences to his own life, so that the patient may give up the damaging pattern and live by his own more particular life-style.

One of the methods of imparting this therapy is to give the patient a model to steer by and emulate. Thus the patient may be taught to take on the patterns of living of the therapist, his clothes, his reactive patterns, his ideas in order to hold onto something strong and healthy while he is in a state of search. After more confidence is his, the patient may begin to locate where his own patterns of living would be and to follow them. He may, for example, be so angry at his parents that he is unable to pick the strong qualities of a parent's behavior to identify with and remobilize in his own life choices. Analysis and therapy can give the patient the opportunity to meet and give vent to the blocking anger so that he is able to move beyond it to the role of healthy identification. The therapist's role in this exercise is to take a neutral non-moral stance and to lead the patient to more options in his behavior, conquering anxiety not by making it disappear but by defending against it with more productive weapons in the personality: the infusion of new defenses for the ego.

These, at least, are some of the things that may happen for the neurotic patient during his therapy. He may have fears of the opposite sex or of his own sex and may have neurotic goals leading him. A group situation may afford him more recognition of a depression which is the product of faulty behavior with other human beings. Group therapy may help to conquer this pattern by showing the patient that he has nothing to fear from other human beings and from giving him an expanded sense of trust in the environment in which he lives. For it is this sense of trust that may have eluded him so poignantly in his infancy and lie at the core of his behavioral difficulties. The impartment of it may become the principal or first task of the therapy or analysis.

During the process of letting this action take place, the psychiatrist himself indulges in what has been called a countertransference. Transference refers once again to the irrational factors in the relationship of the patient to the doctor, the patient behaving toward the analyst or therapist with the feelings and reactions which he felt towards his parents. Being irrational in the situation may serve as the drawing board for all the rest of the therapeutic tasks of understanding. The physician himself engages in a counterreaction which is the reaction with anxiety of his own towards the patient. He is legally charged with some burden of controlling this reaction in himself as he is of leading the patient's transference into coherent paths.

The doctor's task with the psychotic rather than the neurotic patient may be to give him sufficient poles of meaning and feeling to serve as touchstones for rational thinking and feeling. It may be like reaching into a box filled with dry ice to impart an object of reality and trust upon which some adherence to reality can be founded. The doctor must, however, be honest with his feelings and serve as a bastion of trust to the patient. For if the doctor fails in being trustworthy and inevitably on the side of the patient, the entire course of treatment may be ruined.

This is the area in which we begin to chart the responsibility of the psychiatrist imparting therapy or undertaking analysis of his patient. The first and most basic element of the doctor's charge is acting with this sense of imparting trust always guiding and governing the relationship. The relationship between the psychiatrist and his patient is of the most extreme confidence. This is not simply because the things that are talked about are the secrets of the soul but because the patient's continued and embryonic stability may depend upon there being a reliable external source of meaning and later of identification and direction for him.

Without telling the psychiatrist what the words should be,

the literature of psychoanalysis and psychotherapy tells him what his goals should be in the therapy. The role is often strictly set forth.[9]

THE DOCTOR-PATIENT RELATIONSHIP: CERTAIN DUTIES

The inception of the doctor-paitent relationship may lie in a context where the central reliance of the patient may be upon the communication to him by the doctor that he is qualified to undertake the patient's care as being qualified to exert the best of medical skill in the treatment of the patient's condition. On the other hand, the particular issue of whether he is competent and equipped to care for this particular patient's condition cannot be examined or solved until the patient bestows upon the doctor enough trust to describe his condition. This raises issues of capacity upon the physician's part to effect a successful transference and such other preconditions to success which the physician may visualize and be concerned with before undertaking care of the patient.

The first level of communication, then, is presented to the patient implicitly rather than explicitly by the meaning of the sign upon the door, the location of the office and the wearing of white clothes, or most simply by the use of the word "Doctor" before his name. The representation then is communicated not as an obligation of contract or indeed of the entire contract governing their relationship but rather as an express or implied condition precedent to any contractual undertaking between the parties. It is also a representation or warranty which stands in the contract as a clause which may be sued upon and which must occur or exist before any succeeding aspect of the bargain can be enacted. Once the physician undertakes to act in a way which calls for this skill and care obligation (with the obligation to apply both as practiced by the profession in the relevant community), and perhaps also a separable factor of the fiduciary duty of loyalty, then the contract has been breached in the accurate sense of a failure of condition, with the remedy of suit, mutual breach, as for payment of fees to be withheld or counteracting breach.

9 Lower: "The Psychotherapy of Neurotic Dependency," 124 *Amer. J. Psychiat.* 514, 517 (1967).

The patient also has obligations, such as paying his bills regularly, using his best efforts to reach a cure, and respecting the doctor and his integrity and property. To the extent that these are met and the doctor's suggestions not cast aside, the patient may not expect the doctor to foresake him, though if he does depart from these standards enough to make the therapeutic endeavor no longer possible along the doctor's projected course of cure, the doctor may be free to withdraw from the relationship, with probably some duty to offer to refer the patient to another likely physician, always, of course, attempting to make his own reactions as honest as possible. The doctor may have some responsibilities toward the patient even when spurned by him. Although some courts would so argue, the complex of his duties to his patient should not change thereby.

Similarly, when referral is undertaken, the referring physician has a responsibility to forward information to the receiving physician which will be sufficient for him to take over and care for the patient and prevent injury to third parties. When this is not done, and injury is the result, a cause of action may be maintained.[10]

The psychiatrist is the trustee of whatever is given him in terms of the personality, though the relationship has its origin in contract. This contract idea is not a rigid one. Usually it is an oral contract and has many implied terms. It may be evidenced by notes or cards setting down what the patient tells the psychiatrist, or by bills rendered and checks paid. The words at the inception of the relationship regarding fee and duration may be testified to, perhaps by others who are present during the discussion.

But the obligations under the contract are not entirely mutual. The patient, for example, may leave therapy[11] without stating

[10] Underwood v. United States, 356 F.2d 92 (5th Cir. 1966) (liability for patient's killing of his wife).

[11] In a case of rather strong patient orientation, the Georgia Court of Appeals determined that after treatment or examination previously given of a patient has begun, the patient's consent to such treatment or examination, previously given, may be withdrawn so as to subject the doctor to liability for assault and battery if either is continued. *Mims v. Boland,* 138 S.E.2d 902 (Ga. 1964). The leavetaking may be more easily achieved in psychiatric treatment.

terms therefore and probably without incurring liability for the cost of the sessions not attended in the future, though perhaps, if the psychiatrist was not told about it in due course and did not have an opportunity to make other similarly productive arrangements for unattended sessions in the past, he would still be liable, despite the argument that if they are not charged for at the end of the month or the particular governing billing period, right of recovery may have been waived.

Thus, while a patient may perhaps leave therapy without stating terms therefore, the physician might thereafter be liable in malpractice for terminating the therapy on his own if the patient is injured by the withdrawal and the physician has not made all diligent efforts to act as the patient's physician again. If he proved that it would harm the patient or cause him undue pain to have him reenter the therapy, the result might be otherwise.

The onesidedness of the ability to leave or to be responsible is not entire.[12] The physician may, perhaps, have the right to discontinue the therapy if his fee is not paid, or absent reasonable deferrals, there does not appear to be reasonable likelihood of its being paid. Similarly, he may have a right to discontinue therapy if the patient destroys some of his furniture, is uncontrollably destructive to a group undergoing therapy together, or simply does not follow the doctor's orders. This latter condition may be the most telling, for it means that the mutual undertaking to pursue a therapeutic path is no longer being followed, and as such, continuance under a mutual joinder of the spirit[13] in an effort to work behavior change is no longer possible. This latter meaning may be the trust tenet of the relationship and may be

12 This onesidedness may be a reason for calling the relationship contractual only unilaterally. But the joinder of the spirit is the real test of the relationship, the patient having the obligation diligently to apply what is told him.

13 *See* Jaspers, *The Nature of Psychotherapy* 27, 46 (Phoenix ed. 1965).

> Therapeutic effort is limited both by the reality of the environment and by the patient being "thus and no other." Because of this, therapy in the end always becomes some kind of philosophical undertaking. Should it choose to illumine rather than obscure, it will have to teach humility and renunciation as well as the need to grasp at positive possibilities. Obviously this is not something that psychology or medicine can accomplish but only the close collaboration of doctor and patient in a mutual philosophic faith.

Id., p. 27.

the underlying question against which every deviation must be tested.

From this mutuality of engagement springs the test for evaluation of the relationship as having been harmed and the malpractice conclusion having been reached. This is substantially that both doctor and patient must cooperate with the reasonable needs or demands of the other, be they monetary, temporal or emotional. We may understand the "spiritual" as the dedication of will and effort to the achievement of new states of consciousness and to mutually undergo an attempt to reach back over time to the emotional feelings of childhood. The physician may have an obligation to visualize and treat, and thus have a capacity to "accept," the unreasonable demands of the patient, patterns of behavior whose acceptance and whose understanding and replacement by firmer sources of defense constitute so much of the work of the therapy. And in this sense, compassion and optimism are not separable aspects of the psychiatrist's contribution, for in this sense any and every aspect of his own personality may be called upon to aid the patient. Compassion and optimism may be other words for the empathy and reality front which it is the psychiatrist's job to produce and instill in the patient, or rather, it is his job to direct the patient to those sources of perhaps passion or energy and engagement which lie fallow or are misdirected in a depression, for example. Compassion is not a quality of gift or something outside the terms of the therapy. It is central to it—always, of course, given realistically, i.e. when a basis therefore exists in the patient's circumstances. The degree of instillation or the calling for optimism differ in intensity or degree as the patient is unable to visualize the well-springs of these feelings in his own self. The doctor is called upon to realize that the less self-confidence the patient has, the more necessary the doctor's task may be to state the confidence rendering notes or to make statements in terms of almost grandiose or extrahighly tempered comparisons or prophesies.[14] Thus what may be customarily thought of as compassion or optimism may be the very medium of

[14] These may be restated in somewhat less grandiose and more realistic terms when the patient has developed more reality based senses of himself or self estimates.

the therapy itself.[15] It is and should be loanable to the patient or reserved, depending upon therapeutic or medical indication.[16]

It may be that in terms of not abandoning the therapy, the psychiatrist is bound to continue attending the patient until his unreasonable demanding process is at an end.

Further, the psychiatrist may have some obligation to see as unreasonable what the patient may visualize as reasonable, or at least this is so in those cases where one of the patient's symptoms is unrealistic appraisal of events or stimuli, internal or external. This would certainly be so in the treatment of schizophrenia or paranoia, where perceptual capacity is severely hampered. It is this conflict of perception which may precede the abandonment of therapy, destructive events therein, or the filing of a malpractice suit by the patient. The reaction to the demands of the patient depends upon the situation: hospital or otherwise and type and stage of illness. The psychiatrist may thus have positive obligations to visualize an anxiety-free or non-neurotic person if it be there beneath the cloak of these defenses so that he may help to lead the patient to such positive sources of his own identity. As well as having this prevision of the person he shall help to produce, the psychiatrist may have some obligation to be aware of the aspects of life around him which will be adequate and productive areas for long- or short-term investments in identity for the patient.

WHAT IS MALPRACTICE?

Malpractice is a special remedial category designed to regulate professional misfeasance. Its attributes are the measurement of lack of skill and care by a physician in a doctor-patient relationship against a professionally proved standard of community practice. It involves damage caused the patient by the acts of a psychiatrist. It differs thus from ordinary tort law by the existence of a doctor-patient relationship and by proof of the standard of care

15 Jaspers, *op. cit. supra*, p. 46: "Psychotherapy rests on faith but does not create a faith. If the therapist is to preserve his integrity he must be able to accept real faith openly and positively. . . ."

16 The feelings of everyday existence, in their widest coin, are the applications or failures thereof which must be measured against the thermometer of regular medical practice to arrive at a judgment of malpractice.

and its breach by expert testimony. Stripped of this proof, and aside from some minor differences, it resembles conventional negligence in every respect.[17] The chief doctrinal objections to including psychiatry in this concept are the lack of a community standard of care and difficulty in proving injury. The failure of demonstrable proof of injury would shipwreck even a conventional negligence standard.

Malpractice is designed to regulate professions with an established standard of care. It must be an objective one though subjectivity may play a large part in diagnosis and treatment.[18] Medicine conventionally has this attribute of an objective, thoroughly worked out and provable standard. It is generally physiological rather than psychological in analysis and care, as are the injuries that have until recently been freely compensated in tort law. It is because their method and the injuries they have produced and been called forth to answer for, that electroshock and insulin shock therapies rendered under the direction of psychiatrists have been easily included in malpractice. They are akin to medicine's conventional methods and injuries and have regularly been the subject of litigation and recovery. While also under the roof of psychiatry—an aspect of psychiatric practice—they contribute little to the question of whether or not psychoanalysis and psychotherapy can be subjected to malpractice supervision.

Nevertheless, when we speak of whether the use of the shock therapies is called for or not, their medical indication is no different from the prerequisite diagnostic indication for the verbal therapies. We cannot thus differentiate between the diagnostic acts necessarily prerequisite to electroshock therapy and the sort that precedes psychoanalysis, although in the verbal therapies, the

[17] Except the different statutes of limitations and damages. But these are effects rather than attributes. There may also be actions against physicians based upon their special agreements with their patients entered into as consensual relations. Such actions are to be differentiated from malpractice. Stewart v. Rudner, 349 Mich. 459, 84 N.W.2d 816 (1957).

Nevertheless, there are forms of action such as prima facie tort which have not been extended to the doctor-patient relationship. *See* Hammer v. Polsky, 36 Misc.2d 482, 233 N.Y.S.2d 110 (1962).

[18] *See* Seavey: "Negligence Subjective or Objective," 41 *Harv. L. Rev.* 1 (1927).

diagnostic process may shade off imperceptibly into the treatment process.[19] Indeed diagnosis in any theatre of psychiatry—precommitment, competency, criminal responsibility—has not been conventionally[20] repudiated, though its difficulty has been remarked,[21] and even though it has been seen as more subjective than objective and in its intuitive aspects largely different from conventional medical diagnosis.

In pleading a cause of action for malpractice, it is a necessary element of the case that the plaintiff allege the existence of a physician-patient relationship during the time of the alleged injurious episode. Where it is not alleged, the cause of action will be dismissed.[22]

The doctor-patient relationship is one based upon a contract between the two of care and skill within an embryo of confidence. It is based upon a physician's contract to seek the medical welfare of the patient and to pursue the patient's amelioration or cure through the exercise of the care and skill which his medical status promises for the patient. This is not unlike the shingle theory so often imposed to describe the relationship of securities broker to client but involves far more in-depth exposure by patient to doctor. In psychoanalysis, the terms of the contract are balanced. Speaking of the "plan of cure," Freud wrote:

> We form a pact with each other. The sick ego promises us the most complete candor—promises, that is, to put at our disposal

19 *See* Sifneos: "Change in patient's Motivation for Psychotherapy," 128 *Am. J. Psychiat.* 718 (1971):

> Although psychiatric evaluation of the emotional conflicts underlying a patient's symptoms is difficult, it is the only tool that helps us to sort out those individuals whom a specific kind of dynamic psychotherapy is best suited to their idiosyncratic needs. These needs have more to do with the patient's desire for overall emotional behavior and interactions with people than simply with relief of his symptoms. The kind of psychiatric evaluation required to assess such needs is not only difficult but is also complicated, at times, by the notorious lack of clear-cut lines between the end of evaluation and the beginning of treatment.

20 We may differentiate in this regard the views of Thomas Szasz, for example, where the terms of conventional diagnosis have been sharply questioned. Szasz: *The Myth of Mental Illness* (1961).

21 *See* Louisell and Williams: *Trial of Medical Malpractice Cases* § 2.16, p. 50 (1970): "Even the most competent psychiatrist often is unable to discern the chief causes of his patient's disorders and to treat or control them effectively."

22 Hammer v. Polsky, 36 Misc.2d 482, 233 N.Y.S.2d 110 (1962).

all the material which its self-perception yields it; we assure the patient of the strictest discretion and place at his service our experience in interpreting material that has been influenced by the unconscious. Our knowledge is to make up for his ignorance and to give his ego back its mastery over lost provinces of his mental life. This pact constitutes the analytic situation.[23]

[23] Freud, *An Outline of Psycho-Analysis* 30 (1940) (Strachey, ed. 1969).

Chapter II

Aspects of Malpractice In Psychiatry: Problems of Proof

THE STANDARD OF CARE: THE DIFFICULTY OF FORMULATION

Perhaps the most vexing problem with respect to liability for negligence or malpractice in conventional psychotherapy and psychoanalysis is that of fixing a standard of care. In general, the standard is stated to be that of the relevant medical community in which the psychiatrist practices. It is argued, however, that there is no standard sufficient to mark deviance therefrom a breach of duty.[1] There surely are articles, books, certifying boards, training institutes and practitioners, medical faculties and other indicia of a community standard[2] but cases themselves suggest the radical degree of innovation in the area at a time when the new group therapies[3] have moved into a crystallizing standard of care and the consequent shakiness of the standard. In an implicit attempt to make of this shakiness an incident of fraud, it has been suggested that conventional outpatient treatment at conventional prices in this area creates a cause of action for fraud:

In the second cause of action, plaintiff son alleges that while

1 *Cf* Note, 75 *Harv. L. Rev.* 1445, 1447 (1962) observing the lack of clarity of a medical custom on risk disclosure in obtaining consent: "The actual existence of a custom in these circumstances is highly unlikely; even if one did exist, it would necessarily be so general as to be of little value."

2 And also of the qualification of a particular defendant. *See* Hammer v. Rosen, 7 N.Y.2d 376, 165 N.E.2d 756 (1960). *See* Warner v. Packer, 139 App. Div. 207, 208, 123 N.Y. Supp. 725, 727 (1910): "The plaintiff did not advance the proposition that the defendants were not qualified. On the other hand, the evidence shows that they were educated in their profession, alienists who as such had filled important public positions, and were of large experience gained from thousands of examinations."

3 *See* Ruitenbeek: *The New Group Therapies* (1970).

> defendant was treating him for his illness, defendant demanded and received $8,350 which defendant falsely and fraudulently represented to be a fair fee for which he would render certain services; that he did not render such services. There is nothing in defendant's moving affidavit to show that these allegations are sham. Defendant argues that the first and third causes of action are bludgeons to scare him into refunding the money received. Defendant says: "In other words, the plaintiff is not willing to present the clear cut issue to the court as to the adequacy or inadequacy of that payment." But in the second cause of action, plaintiff is trying to do just that—to determine what a fair fee would be and to litigate the question of whether defendant fraudently represented as fair a fee that was excessive. It may be that plaintiff has asked too much in demanding the return of the entire fee paid instead of asking for only the excess above a fair fee, but the sufficiency of a complaint is not determined by the "wherefore" clause. . . . Moreover, plaintiff alleges that defendant did not render the treatments agreed upon. These are questions of fact for determination at the trial.[4]

Similar uneasiness before the charging of large fees by psychiatrists is reflected in *Hammer v. Rosen*[5] where, although a cause of action in fraud was held properly dismissed, the dissent below (adopted by the appellate court) suggested that failure to achieve ameliorative results when large fees are paid establishes worsening of the illness: "It is conceded that at the conclusion of defendant's treatment between 1948 and 1955, involving expenditures of over 55,000 dollars, the condition of the patient plaintiff had not improved. The lack of improvement despite the time lapse establishes regression rather than stabilization of her condition."[6]

[4] Gasperini v. Manginelli, 196 Misc. 547, 550, 92 N.Y.S.2d 575, 577-578 (Sup. Ct. 1949). It may be that such an allegation would less readily occur in conventional medical treatment.

[5] 7 N.Y.2d 376, 165 N.E.2d 756, 198 N.Y.S.2d 65 (1960).

[6] 7 App. Div. 2d 216, 217, 181 N.Y.S.2d 805, 806, *modified* 7 N.Y.2d 376, 165 N.E.2d 756, 198 N.Y.S.2d 65 (1960); *but see* Freud: "Analysis Terminable and Interminable," reprinted in Freud, *Therapy and Technique,* Rieff, ed., N.Y. 1963, p. 233:

> Experience has taught us that psychoanalytic therapy—the liberation of a human being from his neurotic symptoms, inhibitions and abnormalities of character—is a lengthy business. Hence, from the very beginning, attempts have been made to shorten the course of analysis. Such endeavors required no justification: they could claim to be prompted by the strongest considerations alike of reason and expendiency. But there probably lurked in them some trace of the impatient contempt with which the medical profession of an earlier day regarded the neuroses, seeing in them the unnecessary results of invisible lesions.

Unsuccessful though it was, a concomitant action in fraud relating to a promise to cure, was alleged:

> The jury's finding that the defendant, a psychiatrist, had not undertaken by contract to warrant a cure for the plaintiff incompetent of schizophrenia within a few months is entirely justified by the record. The cause of action for fraud, which is closely dependent upon the contract cause, was properly dismissed by the court and is in any event not supported by proof.[7]

There can be no doubt that the uncertainty of cure and the lack of regularization of treatment, whether a justified perception or not, breeds actions in breach of warranty and fraud as practitioners have sometimes been victimized in their attempts to deal with often "intractable forces."[8] Similarly, assurances that patients "will be cared for" often leaves an ambiguity as the prospects for cure or permanent amelioration which a deeply concerned family member might interpret as a warranty. It would be well if clarity of prospect could be pursued.

But the difficulty is not simply the standard of care's formulation. It is also the difficulty of achieving accuracy of diagnostic judgment, especially when prognosis is attempted. Indeed many psychiatrists shrink from and are taught to avoid making detailed or otherwise definite speculations as to the prognosis for any patient. When they do not, they may summon a nest of allegations sounding in breach of warranty or fraud. This says nothing of the crucial role that each patient must play in his own treatment. Magical cure at the hands of the therapist is a hope shared by many patients, but the contribution of the patient in achieving his own cure is an immeasurable but important aspect of treatment.

The courts have persisted in remarking the difficulty of diagnostic and prognostic acts by psychiatrists. In 1910, the Appellate Division of the New York Supreme Court reversed a judgment for malpractice by alienists in a lunacy examination because no

[7] *Id.*, p. 805.

[8] Landau v. Werner, (Q.B. March 7, 1961), in *The Times* (London) March 8, 1961, p. 5, col. 3, *aff'd* (C.A. Nov. 22, 1961) in *The Times* (London) Nov. 23, 1961, p. 5, col. 1.

expert testimony was adduced as to the patient's sanity.[9] Said the Court:[10]

> We know insanity is a mysterious disease, that it may exist without physical indications, is often cunningly concealed so as almost or altogether to baffle detection even by a specialist, or may be so occult as to cause most eminent alienists to clash as to its existence in an instance. The diagnosis of it is recognized as a difficult task. (Balfour Browne, Medical Jurisprudence of Insanity, 320; Mann's Medical Jurisprudence 113.) Wharton & Stille on Medical Jurisprudence (Vol. 1, § 1240): write "In brief, the task of a physician when he examines a patient for certification is to make a diagnosis. If, for any reason, he is not able to make a diagnosis, he should not sign the certificate. The whole art of diagnosis may be involved in the case, and there is no rule for it except to have a reliable knowledge of insanity."

This case was followed and given application in 1954 by the Appellate Division where it was alleged that a negligent diagnosis of capacity to be discharged from a state hospital for the criminally insane caused a killing by the former patient without protection.[11] In reversing a judgment for plaintiff, the court emphasized that the State would not be liable for an honest error in professional judgment by its physicians:[12]

> The diagnosis of mental cases is not an exact science. As yet, the mind cannot be x-rayed like a bone fracture. Diagnosis with absolute precision and certainty is impossible. One of the claimant's experts readily admits having made mistakes in diagnoses; yet says of the Matteawan doctors "They made a mistake." It has been recognized that insanity is difficult of detection and frequently is cunningly concealed. . . . Of necessity it must be a matter of judgment by those qualified to pass judgment.
>
> Future human behavior is unpredictable. . . .The Appellate Division of the New York Supreme Court has even more recently

[9] Warner v. Packer, 139 App. Div. 207, 123 N.Y. Supp. 725 (2d Dept. 1910).
[10] *Id.* at 214, 123 N.Y. Supp. at 731.
[11] St. George v. State, 283 App. Div. 245, 127 N.Y.S.2d 147 (3rd Dept. 1954).
[12] *Id.* at 248, 127 N.Y.S.2d at 150. The court introduced a habeus corpus test on propriety of release from the hospital.

refused to fix liability upon the State for an assault by one of its discharged patients:[13]

> The prediction of the future course of a mental illness is a professional judgment of high responsibility and in some instances it involves a measure of calculated risk. If a liability were imposed on the physician or the State each time the prediction of future course of mental disease was wrong, few releases would ever be made and the hope of recovery and rehabilitation of a vast number of patients would be impeded and frustrated. This is one of the medical and public risks which must be taken on balance, even though it may sometimes result in injury to the patient or others.

ASSUMPTION OF THE RISK AND CONTRIBUTORY NEGLIGENCE

It is significant that statements of the difficulty of diagnosing mental illness occur in the context of violent acts caused by released or escaping hospitalized mental patients. In these situations, the damage caused is large and the defendant often the State. But diagnosis as to the prospects for amelioration of condition is also difficult because of the active role of psychiatric patients in their treatment as opposed to the oftimes comparably passive role of nonpsychiatric medical patients. Magical cure at the hands of the therapist is a hope shared by many patients, but the contribution of the patient himself in achieving his own cure is an immeasurable but important aspect of treatment. The patient must adopt as his own the insights and model of the therapist. He must work himself to understand and to feel a more healthy style of life and thought. The difficulty of comparing and quantifying the roles of doctor and patient as they change from stage to stage and moment to moment contributes to the difficult task of measuring either one's role. Assumption of the risk may be appropriate to account for technical declines in treatment—if the patient is forewarned—and contributory negligence can also, in less likely circumstances, play a part in analyzing failure of cure or amelioration.

The psychiatric patient thus has a difficult and extensive part

13 Taig v. State, 19 App. Div. 2d 182, 183, 241 N.Y.S.2d 495, 496-497 (3rd Dept. 1963).

to play in dealing with his mental illness. Crucial to this concept is motivation for change.[14] Moreover, the very process of developing a healthy identity is an ongoing task of personal creativity which may exist even for the non-neurotic.[15]

THE STANDARD OF CARE: THE MEDICAL MODEL

Nevertheless, it should not be thought that psychiatry does not have standards to be followed by its practitioners merely because they may differ from those applicable in other branches of medicine. In his essay on "The Nature of Clinical Evidence,"[16] Erik H. Erikson has set forth his understanding of how a clinician really works.[17] His description "of the nature of evidence gathered in the psychotherapeutic encounter"[18] reviews "the elements making up the clinical core of medical work" as

> . . . the encounter of two people, one in need of help, the other in the possession of professional methods. Their *contract* is a therapeutic one: in exchange for a fee, and for information revealed in confidence, the therapist promises to act for the benefit of the individual patient, within the ethos of the profession. There usually is a *complaint,* consisting of the description of more or less circumscribed pain or dysfunction, and there are *symptoms,* visible or otherwise localizable. There follows an attempt at an *amaneunsis,* an etiological reconstruction of the disturbance, and an *examination,* carried out by means of the physician's naked senses or supported by instruments, which may include laboratory methods. In evaluating the evidence and in arriving at diagnostic and prognostic infer-

14 *See* Sifneos: "Change in Patient's Motivation for Psychotherapy," 128 *Am. J. Psychiat.* 718 (1971): "A patient's 'motivation for psychotherapy' is a crucial selection and prognostic criterion for psychotherapy, since it has been established that patients who are well motivated at the time of psychiatric evaluation tend to improve as a result of their treatment."

15 Wheelis: "To Be a God," 36 *Commentary* 125 (1963): "I elect to believe our future is unwritten, that we create it as we will." *Id.,* p. 134.

16 Erikson: *Insight and Responsibility,* pp. 49-80 (1964).

17 *Id.,* p. 49.

18 *Id.,* p. 50. *See also* Watson: *Psychiatry for Lawyers* 36 (1968). As to the observation's being concerned with the interaction between the clinician and the patient, *see* Diamond: "The Psychiatrist as a Medical Witness," in *Proceedings AMA-ABA National Medicolegal Symposium* 135 (1965). For standards as to the conduct of the psychiatric diagnosis, see Sullivan: *The Psychiatric Interview* (1954).

ences (which are really the clinical form of a *prediction),* the physician *thinks clinically*—that is, he scans in his mind different *models* in which different modes of knowledge have found condensation: the *anatomical* structure of the body, the *physiological* functioning of body parts, or the *pathological* processes underlying classified disease entities. A clinical prediction takes its clues from the complaint, the symptoms, and the amaneunsis, and makes inferences based on a rapid and mostly preconscious cross-checking against each other of anatomical, physiological and pathological models. On this basis, a *preferred method of treatment* is selected. This is the simplest clinical encounter. In it, the patient lends parts of himself to an examination and as far as he possibly can, ceases to be a person, i.e. a creature who is more than the sum of its organs.

Any good doctor knows, however, that the patient's complaint is more extensive than his symptom, and the state of sickness more comprehensive than localized pain or dysfunction. . . . The treatment is thus [52] not limited to local adjustments; it must, and in the case of a "good" doctor automatically does, include a wider view of the complaint, and entail corresponding *interpretations* of the symptom to the patient, often making the "patient himself" an associate observer and assistant doctor. This is especially important, as subsequent appointments serve a *developing treatment-history* which step-by-step verifies or contradicts whatever predictions had been made and put to test earlier.

This, then, . . . is the traditional core of the clinical encounter, whether it deals with physical or with mental complaints. But in the special case of the *psychotherapeutic encounter,* . . . three items crowd out all the others, namely, *complaint, amaneunsis,* and *interpretation.* . . . [I]n what way can the psychological clinician make his own perception and thought reliable in the face of the patient's purely verbal and social expression, and in the absence of non-verbal supportive instruments? . . . [T]he psychotherapist, in many ways, uses the setting and the terminology of a medical and even a laboratory approach, claiming he comes to an anatomy, a physiology and a pathology of the mind, without matching the traditional textbook clarity of medical science in any way. To put it briefly, the element of subjectivity, both in the patient's complaints and in the therapist's interpretations, may be vastly greater than in a strictly medical encounter, although this element is in principle not absent from any clinical approach.

. . . The psychotherapist [53] shares with any clinician the

Hippocratic fact that hour-by-hour he must fulfill a *contract* with individuals who offer themselves to cure and study. . . . The psychotherapist shares with all clinicians the further requirement that even when facing most intimate and emotional matters, he must maintain intellectual inner contact with his conceptual models, however crude they may be. But more than any other clinician, the psychotherapist must include in his field of observation a *specific self-awareness* in the very act of perceiving his patient's actions and reactions. I shall claim that there is a core of *disciplined subjectivity* in clinical work—and this both on the side of the therapist and of the patient—which it is neither desirable nor possible to replace altogether with seemingly more objective methods—methods which originate, as it were, in the machine-tooling of other kinds of work. How the two subjectivities join in the kind of disciplined understanding and shared insight which we think are operative in a cure—that is the question.

According to Erikson, even the act of interpretation, so crucial to understanding and insight on the part of the patient, cannot be given haphazardly. Using a dream and its interpretation as his primary source material, Erikson goes on to point out the method of pursuit:

> The clinician . . . has no right to test his reconstruction until his trial formulations have combined into a comprehensive interpretation which feels right to him and which promises, when appropriately verbalized, to feel right to the patient. When this point is reached, the clinician usually finds himself compelled to speak in order to help the patient in verbalizing his affects and images in a more communicative manner, and to communicate his own impressions.[19] The evidence is not "all in" if . . . [the therapist] does not succeed in using his own emotional responses during a clinical encounter as an evidential source and as a guide in intervention, instead of putting them aside with a spurious claim to unassailable objectivity. It is here that the prerequisite of the therapist's own psychoanalytic treatment as a didactic experience proves itself essential, for the personal equation in the observer's emotional response is as important in psychotherapy as that of the senses in the laboratory.[20]

The verifiability of interpretations lies thus in the therapist's

[19] *Id.*, p. 71.
[20] *Id.*, p. 73.

self-knowledge as well as in that of the patient. Correctness is thus in part given down from teacher to student in the great chain of analytic encounter:

> The proof of the correctness of our inference does, of course, not always lie in the patient's immediate assent. I have, in fact, indicated how this very dream experience followed an hour in which the patient had assented too much. Rather, the proof lies in the way in which the communication between therapist and patient "keeps moving," leading to new and surprising insights and to the patient's greater assumption of responsibility for himself.[21]

These, then, are the terms for measuring success in treatment, one filled with uncertainty, a modicum of improvement: greater responsibility and less dependency.

21 *Id.*, p. 75.

Chapter III

The Standard of Care: Method of Breach: Words

Remaining silent where there is a duty to speak[1] arises both in not giving sufficient amplitude to the discussion preceding consent as well as it may when needed procedures should be imparted or when a particular type of comment from a psychotherapist is not made. It may be necessary at a given time in the therapy—and perhaps not at other times—to render an interpretation or to cut off a particular type of neurotic habit of speech. Given at the wrong time, a particular interpretation or set of them may misinform a patient as to the meaning or healthiness of a particular type of verbal exercise. A highly intellectual mode of discourse may symbolize a failure to speak forthrightly at the level of emotion. Continued misapplication of such verbal sallies (interpretations and the like) can misdirect the course of therapy and may be actionable.

It is not that single interpretations—delivered one time—may not be negligent, it is simply that they may be necessary mistakes of judgment in the therapeutic interaction. Given over a course of time, interpretations grow into a therapeutic strategy, and while the words themselves may not be prescribed by the community, their thrust and meaning may be very definitely called for as a particular message to be imparted to the patient so he must translate into words definitely prescribed modes of thought and action which call for strict control of the therapist's own patterns of thought and action. Implicit in what the therapist should do is what he must not do, and when he does what he should not in the face of clear doctrine in the psychiatric literature, he may be considered negligent. Consider the following:

> The therapist must analyze rather than react, always redirecting the patient toward autonomy. The potential for growth lies

[1] *See* Carpenter v. Blake, 75 N.Y. 12 (1878).

> within the patient himself, as does the resistance which inhibits it. The therapist can be effective only as he turns attention to the struggle within the patient. To this end, the overriding motivation of the therapist must be to understand. This in no way precludes a warm concern for the patient, but concern is best expressed in the implicit wish for the patient to share in mature satisfactions. The quiet and persistent demonstration of belief in the patient's ultimate capacity to develop his own resources gives him a healthy model for identification and increases the strength of his ego toward the resolution of internal conflicts.[2]

With similar strictness, the literature indicates the difference between supportive and analytically oriented therapy. It indicates that even when supplying balm to wounds of feeling, the therapist must be guided by the therapeutic vision:[3]

> Therapeutic modifications must be introduced with unusual care, for the essence of the patient's defense is to involve the therapist in a gratifying relationship. Any supportive measures required from time to time must be self-limited and directed toward helping the ego regain strength for continued growth. This is particularly true of drug therapy; in this age of pharmacotherapy, the best therapeutic intentions can easily promote chronicity in dependent patients. True support directs the patient toward active endeavors, outside of therapy, through his own resources. A consistent expectation of the patient's ability to achieve does most to reverse regression.

As difficult as such a line of leading may be, the therapist must be judged in his encounters with a malpractice allegation by his own profession's standards as they are translated into verbal action.

It has long been held that instructions to a patient may be a source of malpractice when part of a course of physical treatment, although not so limited by the court. Thus, where instructions were not given as to the proper continued support for a reduced dislocated elbow, it was held in *Carpenter v. Blake*[4] that a jury might decide that this was negligence:

[2] Lower: "The Psychotherapy of Neurotic Dependency," 124 *Amer. J. Psychiat.* 514, 517 (1967).

[3] *Ibid.*

[4] 75 N.Y. 12 (1878).

> It was dangerous to straighten the arm or to move it out of its place, and yet it was left without anything to keep it in place and subject to the risk of being displaced by the excitement of a nervous woman, afflicted with pain and suffering, and liable in her anguish to change the position of the arm. The responsibility of not providing safeguards against the consequences of her imprudence or want of self-control rested with the defendant. Neither a sling, which is a common mode, according to some medical authorities, nor splints, which might have been used, were employed. No measures, in fact, were taken to prevent the joint if actually set from being again dislocated. No intimation, as some of the evidence shows, had been given to those who attended the plaintiff of this great peril, although instructions were asked for and she was left in charge of those who by reason of their ignorance or inexperience might well have neglected to give that care, attention and vigilance, which if proper knowledge and information had been communicated, might have been observed. It is said that Mrs. Miller, who attended the plaintiff, admits the defendant gave directions to "stand and watch." Whether this was sufficient to point out the danger and to guard against reluxation, is not entirely manifest, as the language employed conveyed no information of the nature of the difficulty which might ensue or how to guard against it. If there was a negligent omission in the particulars indicated, or unskillfulness, the liability of the defendant was the same. Proper instructions may have avoided much of the suffering to which the plaintiff was subjected and prevented the serious consequences which followed.[5]

It was intimated[6] in *Carpenter v. Blake* that a physician would be liable for negligent advice given to a patient after his discharge. It was objected that the trial court mistakenly allowed a question put to plaintiff asking whether she relied on what the doctor told her about the condition of her arm at the various times he examined it. Said the Court:

> [W]hether he really was in the case continuously or otherwise, there could be no objection to the question. If what was said in regard to the condition of the arm misled the plaintiff in respect to the importance of giving it additional attention and prevented her employing a surgeon for that purpose, no reason is apparent why he should not be responsible for the conse-

5 75 N.Y. at 18-19.

6 International Products Co. v. Erie R. Co., 244 N.Y. 331, 337, 155 N.E. 662 (1927).

> quences which followed. The defendant had been her original medical attendant and advisor, and it was reasonable to suppose even if he had not continued treating her after he had left the case, that his advice would be followed. That she believed what he did say as to the condition of the arm is an excuse for not knowing that the arm was improperly set, and if it was not, for not using other means to secure the proper treatment to remedy the difficulty. Nor is it an answer, we think, to the considerations suggested that the plaintiff was or had been under the charge of another surgeon or that the conversations between the plaintiff and the defendant were more of a friendly character and not while the defendant acted in a professional capacity.
>
> * * * *
>
> If by reason of the defendant's ignorance or his negligence he had induced the plaintiff to rest quiet and lulled her into security so that she was misled or deceived and failed to employ a surgeon in due season or to use the necessary precautions to prevent the joint from being displaced after he had as claimed set the same, it would seem but just that the defendant should be liable for such misleading and deception.[7]

The case raises the crucial issue by suggesting that duties may arise or at least continue—physician to patient—without prior, or at least after termination of, contractual relations between physicians and patients:[8]

> It is also insisted that the request to charge, "that if the defendant gave advice to the plaintiff after his discharge without being employed by her, and entitled to compensation, he was not responsible," should have been charged without the qualification "and did not mislead or deceive her," added by the judge. We think that there was no error in this respect. The defendant had been employed as the plaintiff's surgeon, and unfortunately by reason of his want of skill, or for some other cause, she has sustained serious injury. The proof tended to show that it was attributable to malpractice on his part, and if in interviews after he had been discharged, he gave advice which was wrong and which tended to mislead and deceive her, I think he was responsible for such advice. He thereby assumed to act on her behalf, and no valid reason exists why he should not be liable for the act.

[7] 75 N.Y. at 21-22.

[8] 75 N.Y. at 24. This occurred even in the context of the infinitely more segregable acts of surgery and comment as opposed to a situation where every word is itself therapeutically spoken.

THE DUTY TO SPEAK SKILLFULLY AND CAREFULLY AND THE NEGLIGENT USE OF WORDS

In the ordinary activities of man, there is no general duty to speak skillfully and carefully or even accurately. Cases of slander aside, there is ordinarily no liability for the negligently spoken word.[9] Exception to this rule applies where the words spoken are "more than a representation" but "constitute a verbal act" which is part and parcel of a "special relationship"[10] arising out of contract or fiduciary relationship.[11] Duty arising out of such relationship obligates the speaker, if he speaks at all, to give the correct information.[12] For the obligation to exist, there must be (a) "knowledge," or its equivalent, that the information is "desired" for a "serious purpose";[13] (b) that he to whom it is given "intends" to "rely" and "act" upon it;[14] (c) that if false and erroneous, the plaintiff will be "injured" thereby; and (d) that the relationship of the parties, "arising" out of "contract" or "otherwise"[15] must be such that in "morals and good conscience"[16] the one had the "right to rely" upon the other for "information"[17] and that he who gives the information owes a duty to "give it with care."[18] *Glanzer v. Shepard*[19] had limited the instant liability to an "act in the law" rather than merely to "careless words":[20]

[9] Dorsey Products Corp. v. United States Rubber Corp., 21 App. Div. 2d 866, 251 N.Y.S.2d 311 (1967), *aff'd*, 16 N.Y.2d 925, 212 N.E.2d 435 (1965) (product liability in a distributorship agreement relating to polyesters); Glanzer v. Shepard, 233 N.Y. 236, 135 N.E. 275 (1922); International Prod. Co. v. Erie R. Co., 244 N.Y. 331 (1927).

[10] *Ibid.*

[11] Jaillet v. Cashman, 235 N.Y. 511, 139 N.E. 714 (1923) (negligent publication of news over ticker).

[12] International Prod. Co. v. Erie R. Co., 244 N.Y. 331 (1927).

[13] *Id.* at 338.

[14] *Ibid.* "The inquiry must be made as the basis of independent action" *Ibid.* and there must be faith in the accuracy of the words.

[15] *Ibid.* The case seeks to encompass more than a fiduciary relationship. See, note 11 *supra.*

[16] *Ibid.* These words are suggestive of equitable right.

[17] *Ibid.* The concept of the verbal act suggests that the idea of information is to be taken broadly within the context of the other strictures of the doctrine.

[18] *Ibid.*

[19] 233 N.Y. 236, 135 N.E. 275 (1922).

[20] *Id.* at 239-241, 135 N.E. at 276.

> It is ancient learning that one who assumes to act, even though gratuitously, may thereby become subject to the duty of acting carefully, if he acts at all. . . . [The] principle applies . . . where action is directed toward the governance of conduct. . . . Here the defendants are held, not merely for careless words . . ., but for the careless performance of a service—the act of weighing—which happens to have found in the words of a certificate its culmination and its summary. . . .

The relevance and application of this concept to the physician, and especially to the psychiatrist has interlaced the process of deriving the concept of words negligently spoken as it has future application of the doctrine. *International Products*[21] overrode English hesitancy to recognize the doctrine:[22]

> The denial, under all circumstances, of relief because of the negligently spoken or written word, is, it is said, a refusal to enforce what conscience, fair dealing, and the usages of business require. The tendency of the American courts has been toward a more liberal construction. The searcher of a title employed by one who delivers his abstract to another to induce action on the faith of it must exercise care. . . . So must a physician who assures a wife that she may safely treat the infected wound of her husband *(Edwards v. Lamb,* 69 N.H. 599, 45 A. 480, 50 L.R.A. 160) or, hired by another, examines a patient and states the result of his diagnosis *(Harriott v. Plimpton,* 166 Mass. 585, 44 N.E. 992). . . .
>
> In New York we are already committed to the American as distinguished from the English rule. In some cases, a negligent statement may be the basis for a recovery of damages. A reference is made to the question in *Carpenter v. Blake,* 75 N.Y. 12. We intimated that a physician would be liable for negligent advice given to a patient after his discharge, but this suggestion was not decisive of the point we now consider.[23]

Since *International Products,* a complaint has been held sufficient against a physician for the verbal act of negligently "selecting" and "recommending" an operating surgeon who was incompetent and unskillful to the knowledge of the defendant at the time he selected and recommended him to the decedent.[24] A

[21] International Prod. Co. v. Erie R. Co., 244 N.Y. 331, 155 N.E. 662 (1927).

[22] *Id.* at 336, 155 N.E. at 663.

[23] *Id.* at 336-337, 155 N.E. at 663.

[24] Cestone v. Harkavy, 243 App. Div. 732, 277 N.Y.S. 438 (1935) (wrongful death.)

psychiatrist has been held liable for consequent damages following the impartment of his diagnosis[25] or of confidential information gained during treatment [26] to third parties.

These cases suggest a variety of situations where there has arisen a habit of holding physicians, including psychiatrists, liable for negligent use of the spoken word.

If we measure the psychoanalytic method of providing medical therapy by the skillful use of the spoken word against the cases which define the doctrine of words negligently spoken, the requisite factors may be found to exist. The dangers that inaccurate, careless or inapposite words may be applied[27] by psychiatrists

[25] Berry v. Moench, 8 Utah 2d 191, 331 P. 2d 814 (1958). In *Moench,* a physician had diagnosed and treated the plaintiff six years before. He imparted his diagnosis to another physician whose stated purpose of inquiring was to pass it on to the parents of a young woman who was then keeping company with the plaintiff. A jury question was presented as to whether defendant had exercised proper discretion in relation to the school of practice. Damages related to the young woman's disownment by her parents, for though the diagnosis was of manic depression in a psychopathic personality, the woman married plaintiff.

One writer has seized upon some rather broad words in the opinion to suggest that "any" injury suffered by such disclosure would be compensable. *See* Schwartz: "Civil Liability For Causing Suicide: A Synthesis of Law and Psychiatry," 24 *Vanderbilt L. Rev.* 217, 247 (1971); *compare* Hammer v. Polsky, 36 Misc. 2d 482, 233 N.Y.S.2d 110 (1962) (testimony in a custody proceeding privileged).

See also Harriott v. Plimpton, 166 Mass. 585, 44 N.E. 992 (1896), where a physician's informing a third party of a negligent diagnosis of gonorrhoea entitled plaintiff to damages for the breakup of an engagement even though the purpose of the examination was information and not medical treatment. A malpractice standard of proof was applied, though the court spoke in terms of negligence.

[26] Furniss v. Fitchett, [1958] N.Z.L.R. 396; see Hammer v. Polsky, 36 Misc. 2d 482, 233 N.Y.S.2d 110 (1962).

[27] It is not the business of prophylactic treatment to produce the same dangerous situation as that of the illness itself but only something much more mild, as in the case of vaccination and many similar procedures. Similarly, in the analytic prophylaxis of instinctual conflicts, the only methods which we need really consider are . . .: the artificial production of new conflicts in the transference (conflicts which lack the character of reality) and the rousing of such conflicts in the imagination of the patient by talking to him about them and telling him that they may possibly arise.

> . . . We may incite him to jealousy or inflict upon him the pain of disappointed love, but no special technical design is necessary for that purpose. These things happen spontaneously in most analyses. But in the second place, we must not overlook the fact that any such deliberate procedure would necessitate unkind behaviour on the part of the analyst towards the patient and this would have an injurious effect upon his affectionate attitude towards the analyst, i.e. upon the positive transference, which is the patient's strongest motive for co-operating in the work of analy-

caution against mistakes in their application. Thus, invoking the criteria of *International Products*,[28] the psychiatrist knows that his patient desires the informational and other therapeutic effects of the words; that he intends to act upon them; that injury will follow if there is sufficient inaccuracy to the words spoken; the relationship is one of the highest fiduciary caste, creating the highest form of justifiable reliance; and pursuant to his professional status, the psychiatrist has a duty to speak with due care.

But even if a non-malpractice route to liability would seem to be posed by the doctrine of words negligently spoken, it is likely that a court would require expert testimony to corroborate plaintiff's testimony.[29] Thus, these cases may be applied in the malpractice context to indicate that mere words used by a physician in or relating to his treatment may be the subject of malpractice liability.

Indeed, the cases establishing the duty of the careful use of words describe verbal acts even less continuous and central to the activity negligently performed than psychotherapy where the very medium of activity is the ameliorative word. The doctrine would also apply to the certificate of insanity or mental illness and to diagnosis and inducement of consent. If the concept has now been limited to "verbal acts" (instead of mere representations) where

---

> sis. So we shall not form any high expectation of the results of such a technique.

Freud: "Analysis Terminable and Interminable," *Int. J. Psycho-Anal.*, 18 (1937), 373, reprinted Freud, *Therapy and Technique*, Rieff, ed., p. 233, 250-251 (1963).

But, see, Amer. Psychiatric Assn.: Task Force Report. *Encounter Groups and Psychiatry*, p. 12 (1970):

> At the other extreme, there is a tendency to ignore or to disregard rather compelling evidence of adverse consequences of the encounter group experience. . . . [M]any nonclinically trained leaders reject the medical or psychiatric definition of adverse effect; they may assert that the stressing of members to the point of experiencing such extreme discomfort that they require professional help is not a danger but an accomplishment of the encounter group and that these individuals, although they may temporarily appear worse, have in fact undergone a growth experience and will in the long run be more fully integrated individuals. The most extreme view holds, with Laing, that even a psychotic episode may be a growth experience which permits the individual to liberate himself and to realize his potential more fully. In some quarters, this comes close to the advocacy of psychotic experience as a desideratum of personal growth.

28 *See,* text at notes 10-18 *supra.*

29 *See* Beaumont v. Morgan, 427 F.2d 667 (1st Cir. 1970). See p. 61, infra.

some "special relationship" supports the cause of action,[30] psychotherapy is, if anything, the rendering of medical treatment by use of words,[31] the verbal act, supported by the special relationship of doctor and patient, a relationship of the keenest fiduciary nature.

Thus we may see in *Dorsey Products Corp. v. U. S. Rubber Corp.*[32] and may take from the concept of words negligently spoken, in the verbal act of therapy and in the "special relationship" of psychiatrist and patient, a duty upon the psychiatrist to speak skillfully and carefully to his patient.

A psychiatrist, and perhaps any doctor, owes a patient, and perhaps even a non-patient, a duty to speak skillfully and carefully during or about any aspect of his treatment. Depending upon the type of treatment—whether for perceptual incapacity or lack of masculine or feminie identity—he must (even in his "small talk") speak skillfully and carefully about any subject which is discussed as a treatment medium.

The case of *Carpenter v. Blake* suggests that he must speak skillfully and carefully even to non-patients where his authority or skill is being relied on by a person who will, because of his reliance, not undertake independent verification.

It is not just that he must speak or remain silent when he is a psychiatrist, but he must by his speech in the verbal therapies, pursue a curative or therapeutic process by his words, demonstrations of feeling and gesture and even psychiatric leads by the

30 Dorsey Products Corp. v. U. S. Rubber Corp., 21 App. Div. 2d 866, 251 N.Y.S.2d 311 (1964), *aff'd* 16 N.Y.2d 925, 212 N.E.2d 435 (1965).

31 We may distinguish giving information, instructions as to behavior and interpretation. There are diagnostic words, explanations of thought or behavior, suggestions as to action and information about medical or non-medical facts. The cases include words spoken directly to patients and words spoken to third parties who in turn relay them to the patient and thus cause his injury by knowing they have been imparted to a third party or to this particular third party; words transmitted to third parties which reach the patient through other than the original transmittee of the words; and words not spoken when there was a duty to speak, as where silence implies affirmance as for example where an accusation about the patient is made in the physician's presence and the physician remains silent. All varieties of word and silence occur in psychotherapy, with significance varying. We thus might anticipate distinctions between these varieties as the case law unfolds.

32 Note 30 *supra*.

smallest tips—especially where a patient places meaning in every gesture. That is what differentiates a direction or prescription as to how often to take pills from psychotherapy.

The cases specifically dealing with a psychiatrist adhere to this conclusion even while they do not talk in terms of the negligently spoken word. But the words spoken to obtain consent, the speaking in breach of the psychiatrist-patient privilege, the statement of a diagnosis, sometimes the failure to relate facts about a patient to a third person and the certification of insanity (although not directed to the patient himself while he suffers the harm) all rest inherently on the duty to speak carefully either to the patient or to third persons.

THE CONCEPT OF CURE IN PSYCHIATRY

One of the major considerations in fixing liability upon the psychiatrist for his care is to understand correctly what the objects and limits of his treatment are, so that he may in full contractual awareness, rather than as an act of encouragement, contract to pursue a cure of his patient. Such words of prediction may be alien to the psychiatric course of treatment, while in good conscience he may assume or hope that based upon his knowledge of similar cases a full achievement of mental health is possible. The literature abounds in cases where the doctor has failed to reverse a set of symptoms and a course of behavior which it had been his hope to eliminate.[33] This is particularly the result of inadequacies in the science, non-negligent incompatibility between therapist and patient[34] as well as the result of the impalpable nature of much of the patient's resistance.[35]

Furthermore, it is clear that the line between sickness and health with respect to emotional life is not very definite. Achiev-

[33] *See* Louisell and Williams: *Trial of Medical Malpractice Cases* § 2.16, p. 50 (1970).

[34] *See* Louisell and Williams, *op. cit. supra,* § 3.10, p. 85: "A shrewd psychiatrist will endeavor to recognize potentially harmful incompatibilities between himself and his patient and take steps to have the patient treated elsewhere when they appear."

The psychiatrist who falls below the applicable standard of care in recognizing and dealing with such incompatibilities may be liable in malpractice.

[35] Freud: "Analysis Terminable and Interminable," reprinted in Freud, *Therapy and Technique,* (Rieff, ed.), N.Y. 1963, p. 247-248.

ing amelioration of condition may in part thus have to do with making a patient able to tolerate periods of anxiety, depression or elation without the necessity of visiting the psychiatrist constantly. Thus the issue of termination of therapy has much to do with restoring or bringing a patient to a position where he can live relatively comfortably with whatever may be his own handicap. Termination should probably then come at a time when there is a balance between the patient's independence and the fear that more prolonged treatment may render him forever dependent upon psychiatric care. Misjudging this moment of balance may lock the patient into lifelong dependency and, while being a very difficult judgment, may be reviewable legally for the psychiatrist's misjudgement of the possibilities of chronic dependence upon him.[36] He too must judge this moment with sufficient awareness of dependency upon the patient or fear of the patient's getting sick again, which his countertransference may breed. Certainly, factors of financial benefit should not deter him from releasing the patient. These factors must also be taken into account in reducing the frequency of visits or in any other diminution or indeed magnification of dependency. Merely because all of these factors were misjudged at the outset of treatment should not render the psychiatrist liable in malpractice so long as he has a fundamental awareness of them and attempts with his skill to take them into account at the outset of the relationship when he gives prognostication.

It is clear that in *Landau v. Werner,*[37] an inability to resolve the transference after it had been favorably introduced and manipulated was a large cause of the patient's ultimate return to depression and an attempted suicide. Among other factors in the

36 *See,* e.g., Landau v. Werner (Q.B. March 7, 1961) in *The Times* (London) March 8, 1961, p. 5, col. 3, *aff'd* (C.A. Nov. 22, 1961) in *The Times* (London) Nov. 23, 1961, p. 5, col. 1:

> By early April, 1951, things had gone too far to be put right by any course of conduct which Dr. Werner could have adopted. They culminated in the suicide attempt and the suicide note.
>
> The rest of the history consisted of voluminous correspondence written by Miss Landau describing her feelings in tragic terms. She went to other doctors. . . . His Lordship attached no blame to Dr. Werner for making a last attempt to resolve the transference in 1951, as that was done at the express wish of another doctor.

37 Note 36, *supra.*

case, this accounted, whether explicit or not, for the court's judgment:

> Miss Alice Landau was sent to defendant Dr. Theodore Alfons Werner, a psychiatrist, by her own physician in March, 1949. She was in a highly nervous condition and an extremely emotional state. Twenty-four consultations took place at Dr. Werner's consulting rooms. By May 28, 1949, Miss Landau had become emotionally aroused by the treatment, and sexually aroused by the intimate conversations with Dr. Werner. She had feelings of shame and bafflement at the way her affection had developed.
>
> Miss Landau and Dr. Werner discussed her feelings toward him at an interview. Dr. Werner advised her to continue with the treatment, telling her that her feelings of love and bondage would cease. The feelings were "perhaps inherent" in treatment by transference, where past emotion was reactivated and attached to the psychiatrist, causing the patient to feel toward him hopes, desires and fears of the past. Miss Landau accepted the doctor's advice and agreed to continue with the treatment.
>
> The stage was reached where the woman was much "in love," but "so much better in health." The two here came almost to the parting of the ways . Dr. Werner thought, by August of 1949, that Miss Landau was not wholly cured, though much better. He feared that if she were removed from his influence, she might have a relapse and return to the state of anxiety neurosis with which she started in April. He therefore decided not to end his association with Miss Landau. Instead, he embarked on a series of social visits with Miss Landau, including visits to restaurants, trips in taxicabs, one visit to her one-room apartment, and some talk of taking a holiday together.[38]
>
> Dr. Werner did not carry the relationship beyond this. Miss Landau, on the other hand, got much worse. Dr. Werner was attempting to terminate the relationship, but resumed treatment in March of 1950. He sent Miss Landau for some electro-convulsive therapy, to no avail. By April of 1951, things had gone too far for him to put right and she attempted suicide. She went to other doctors, one of whom returned her to Dr. Werner again for an unsuccessful attempt to resolve the transference.

The Court of Appeal was persuaded that all the medical evidence condemned social contacts and found that the trial court

38 These may be understood, if undertaken earlier in treatment, as attempts to establish rapport and the transference.

was justified in its view that in the circumstances, the treatment was likely to have ill effects. It did not quarrel with the trial court's view that Dr. Werner might have terminated the relationship with Miss Landau at the point where he introduced the social relationship, since she then felt that she could probably be able to stand on her own feet, though she was not perfectly cured.

The law of *Landau v. Werner* is not novel. Placing the burden of justifying "unusual and unestablished" treatment upon a defending physician, taking medical expert testimony as its standard of condemnation for such social contacts and judging causation by the likelihood of producing ill effects are settled methods of disposition. But the invocation of such principles in the context of psychotherapeutic malpractice leaves some loose ends. For the Court of Appeal, Dr. Werner's course, after discovering that his patient had fallen in love with him, was to abandon the therapy: "It seemed now that the most prudent thing for Dr. Werner to have done was to refer Miss Landau back to her own doctor and advise that treatment was not completed and should be resumed with someone else." It is settled, however, that the evocation of feelings such as those which Miss Landau experienced is not the signal for termination of a relationship of psychiatrist and patient. On the contrary, such intensity of feeling is not only the mark of some therapeutic success but the prelude to insight on the part of the patient. Such revocation of childhood's repressed intensity of feeling allows the intellectual and emotional examination of feelings not previously understood or dealt with. It is through such reexamination that the emotional learning of psychotherapy takes place. The court seems to have been only partially aware of this process: "She was ashamed and baffled at the way her affection had developed towards a married man with two children. It was something that was perhaps inherent in the system of treatment of transference." The court suggests, however, that the breaking off of the relationship, in the words of the trial court, or referring her back to her own doctor, as the Court of Appeal put it, was the correct, seemingly the only, medically indicated step at the time. It questioned Dr. Werner's judgment that a relapse might follow removal from his influence at the point in question and, with the benefit of hindsight, saw the hazards of the social contacts as of potentially greater magnitude.

Dr. Werner's course of decision might have been given more extended scrutiny. The social visits appear to have been his attempt to find a therapeutic solution to the patient's dependency needs and the independence to be fostered in the therapy. Her individual identity and self-esteem could be supported by the placing of the therapy on a social plane. Though the lower court seems to have seen the social visits as distinct from the therapy, the Court of Appeal and Dr. Werner himself saw them as service to the therapeutic end.

As a solution to the problem of creating independence while preserving a launching pad of dependency, the social visits apparently failed. Perhaps damages are the justified price for innovation that fails. But why was termination of the relationship the appropriate step for Dr. Werner, the course of treatment against which his own path was measured?[39] Why was continued but less frequent therapy not the answer? We are not clearly to understand that the patient, Miss Landau, sought the termination of the relationship at the point where her doctor made the social contacts. There is no suggestion of financial stricture upon continuation of the treatment. Why does the court bind itself to a therapeutic answer which we gather is not even testified to by experts as the correct medical step? Surely a sound basis for criticism of judgment must take the measure of alternatives.

The case is interesting because it holds in substance that every act which a psychiatrist employs in dealing with his patients is subject to legal stricture. While such settings might not now be considered taboo for therapists, the case still stands for making the canons of the medical profession guides and even rules for psychiatric activity. What they may have overlooked is the use of the social visits by the doctor in order to resolve the transference by slowly bridging the gap between deep dependency and an autonomy which would no longer require psychiatric care. The

39 The *Landau* court was especially sensitive to the fact that the psychiatrist pursued the relationship after the patient had made known her intention to leave. Certainly a duty to warn of the consequences of departure arose on his part. Whether a duty to follow her also arose is open to qusetion.

failure to present this view to the court is therefore curious and was fatal to the defense.

By holding that a psychiatrist is answerable for his every act with the patient, the case suggests the evaluation of every word and emotive device as potentially tortious. But new methods have begun to change the scheme of treatment. Thus the new group therapies have been led by the so-called encounter groups to see physical touching, which had been suggested as being improper, as indeed the very medium of the treatment. (Thus while attempting to add physical therapeutic treating to the list of proscribed treatments—as if, said a court, they could never have conceivably been advanced as treatments—it had been implied that certain kinds of physical touching were assault and battery or malpractice *per se.*) Thus many varieties of touching have been utilized to accomplish therapeutic objectives and the evocation of deep fears and other responses which such activity had fostered made clear the need for some regulation.

Since the encounter groups were often led by non-psychiatrists, the feeling was that malpractice remedies were unavailable. It is asserted here that the remedies of negligence or fraud and perhaps breach of contract are nonetheless available and that encounter groups may not go unchecked.

It remains to observe that co-therapists are to be governed by the facts of their participation in a group and be charged with malpractice or negligence by their omission to intervene as well as by their tortious interventions. The field is changing, and we may be awaiting a wealth of litigation in this area.

We shall now look more closely at aspects of psychiatric malpractice that we have just touched upon.

Chapter IV

The Standard of Care: Fiduciary Duty

In substance, the doctor-patient relationship is one of the most profound fiduciary responsibility. It involves a mutual sharing of the deepest feeling and awareness. Its basis is the assured trust of the patient in the care, skill and loyalty of the physician to his emotional well-being. This skill is promised and expected to be that of like psychiatrists practicing in his psychiatric community. This care is expected to be similarly conforming to the needs of the particular therapy he is pursuing. He is also bound to pursue the emotional best interest of the patient he is treating, and he must, in group treatments, for example, carefully choose his words and acts so that he mediates toward the best interest of each individual patient, as of the group. This loyalty means that he will permit no selfish interest of his own or of another patient to divert him from any one patient's or the group's psychiatric needs. This is a task expected of every licensed physician and is the common-law duty of any person vested as are even the non-physician or non-Ph.D. encounter leaders with the deepest emotional dependency of their patients or clients. It is a mutual trust of beneficiary to fiduciary and of fiduciary to beneficiary.

This aspect of trust was the primary underpinning of the malpractice action at common law. It is the primary aspect of a psychiatric patient's getting well. It must be especially defined with care when a minor patient is entrusted to the care of a psychiatrist by his parents. When the interest of the parent and the patient tend to defy congruence, the psychiatrist or other therapist must seek means to pursue that of the patient or perhaps be called upon to discontinue the therapy and refer the patient to someone else.

It has long been recognized that a physician is in a fiduciary relationship with his patient.[1] Not only is this characterization doctrinally necessary for certain legal responsibilities[2]—the duties of skill, care,[3] and loyalty and perhaps also the privileged communication doctrine—but it is essential to the understanding of the relationship of doctor and patient in the practice of certain if not all aspects of psychiatry.[4] It means that if the patient is to get well or for the therapy to provide amelioration of his condition, he must learn to feel secure with the therapist, to place his confidence in him, and pursue the work of therapy with the assurance that the physician is out to benefit him, will keep his confidences and will be sensitive to his needs and pursue them. Confidentiality of communication is only one prerequisite to treatment. It sets the stage for an exchange of thought, word and action at the emotional level. Without trust, there can be no proper transference. In fact, the essence of much psychotherapy is the learning of trust in the external world by the formation of a trusting relationship with the therapist. This becomes the model for trust in the external world and ultimately in the self. It becomes, then, the task of both physician and patient early in the relationship to establish this bond and to make of the therapeutic interaction a theatre of trusting interchange where psychiatrist and patient set forth together on the exploration and amelioration of emotional disturbance. It is clear in the literature that although patients may perceive the process as a cure imparted by a godlike figure—the therapist—in reality, the curative process is a deep emotional interchange among trusting equals who labor together to effect trust, identification, clarity and neutral separation.

[1] Note, 75 *Harv. L. Rev.* 1445 (1962); McCoid, "The Care Required of Medical Practitioners," 12 *Vand. L. Rev.* 549, 586-91 (1959); Sevier: "The Hazards of Medical Treatment: The Duty to Inform and the Right to Know," *Proceedings of ABA Section of Insurance, Negligence and Compensation Law* 396, 398 (1967). These sources recognize the duty in the context of consent. It is here suggested that the duty may also be seen in the context of psychiatric care. *But see* Hunt v. Bradshaw, 242 N.C. 517, 88 S.E.2d 762 (1965).

[2] There is the suggestion of the requirement for words negligently spoken.

[3] Arguably, these first two duties obtain even without the precise characterization as a fiduciary, but it is argued here that the use of the term clarifies analysis.

[4] It is arguable that shock treatments do not require the bond of trust. A question remains as to the giving of consent for shock treatments.

This has been amply noted by psychiatric literature.[5]

In general, courts have been ready to find a fiduciary relationship where power or control has been vested in a second party and an expectation of trust and confidence induced or reposed in the first as a function of the status or relationship or perhaps by particular contract. In the fiduciary relationship of doctor and patient, the early cases allowed court intervention into the doctor-patient relationship when undue influence had

5 "A major goal, especially in the early stage of psychotherapy, is to build a relationship in which the patient comes to trust the doctor as a reliable object." Burnham: "Separation Anxiety," 13 *Arch Gen. Psychiat.* 346, 356 (1965).

> The therapist's model function is salient in his manner of handling major separation from the patient. In general, a matter-of-fact calm trust in the patient's internal resources is helpful, in contrast to an attitude which conveys an uncomfortable, guilt-tinged, fearful concern that the patient may be adversely affected by the separation.

Id. at 357.

This, then, is the application of the therapeutic concept of trust to a specific category of illness. As a characterization of the relationship of psychotherapist and patient and of the specific impartment of a therapy, the concept of trust shares viability at different levels. But basic to all is the total concept of trust in human development of which these are but the specific reflection.

> *See generally* Erikson: 1 *Psychol. Iss.* 50-63 (1959).
> For the first component of the healthy personality, I nominate a sense of basic trust, which I think is an attitude toward oneself and the world derived from the experiences of the first year of life. By "trust" I mean what is commonly implied in a reasonable trustfulness as far as others are concerned and a simple sense of trustworthiness as far as oneself is concerned. When I say "basic," I mean that neither this component nor any of those that follow are, either in childhood or in adulthood, especially conscious. In fact, all of these criteria, when developed in childhood and when integrated in adulthood, blend into the total personality. Their crisis in childhood, however, and their impairment in adulthood are clearly circumscribed.

Id. at 55-56.

"What we call "trust" coincides with what Therese Benedek has called "confidence." If I prefer the word "trust," it is because there is more naivete and more mutuality in it. . . ." *Id.* at 61.

> At any rate, the psychiatrists, obstetricians, pediatricians and anthropologists, to whom I feel closest, today would agree that the firm establishment of enduring patterns for the balance of the basic trust over basic mistrust is the first task of the budding personality and therefore first of all a task for maternal care. . . . Mothers create a sense of trust in their children by that kind of administration which in its quality combines sensitive care of the baby's individual needs and a firm sense of personal trustworthiness within the trusted framework of their community's life style.

Id. at 63.

been exerted.[6] The struggle in defining the duty in each case is to mark out where a court should intervene, and the bastion of non-intervention is respectively the business judgment rule in corporate affairs and the medical judgment rule in the law of physician and patient. According to these rules, some matters fall outside the ambit of the duty of trust and are better left to the unencumbered autonomous authority of the fiduciary.

It is important to note, however, in defining the meaning and scope of the trust concept that it is in either case a legal fiction.[7] The fiction of the trust measures the responsibility of the director or physician rather than the relationship of the one to the corporation, the other to the patient.[8] But unlike the formal trust, there are case-by-case definitions of conduct rather than an established and fully worked out set of specific proscriptions. But there are guides and these must be followed.

Thus it has been stated that a fiduciary should prefer the interests of the beneficiary to his own; that he cannot "serve himself first and his beneficiary second"; and that his standard of behavior must approach if not be "not honesty alone, but the punctilio of an honor the most sensitive."[9] Others have stated the duty in terms followed by at least one test of fiduciary responsibility in the context of the law of corporations: ". . . the physician must act in good faith for the utmost benefit of his patient."[10] To this concept should probably be added the idea of "medical" benefit. This is also stated by the professional ethics of the medical profession.

In psychiatry, the duty of loyalty virtually fuses with that of due care and skill, for the method of treatment in the psycho-

[6] The doctrine was similarly used in the early corporate cases. Indeed there are many similarities in the fiduciary relations of director and corporation and that of doctor and patient for each respectively has at his command the money or physical health of the other person.

[7] *See* Harper and James: *Torts,* 1 §7.13 (1956).

[8] *Ibid.*

[9] Meinhard v. Salmon, 249 N.Y. 458, 164 N.E. 545, 546 (1928).

[10] Sevier, *op. cit. supra,* p. 399. This is the so-called "good faith" test. Others include "fairness." The author notes that the duty of informed consent is derived from this fiduciary setting.

therapies demands the formation and sustaining of a relationship where the highest trust and confidence is observed:

> Patients will be helped only if they can form a trusting relationship with the psychiatrist. Psychotherapy becomes otherwise an ineffective and intellectual exercise. Problems in malpractice involve either a breach of this relationship by the doctor or an unusually faulty approach to the patient's problems.
>
> * * * *
>
> [The patient] is expected to bring up all manner of socially unacceptable instincts and urges, immature wishes, perverse sexual thoughts—in short, the unspeakable, the unthinkable, the repressed. To speak of such things to another human requires an atmosphere of unusual trust, confidence and tolerance.[11]

Thus a failure to observe the trust on the part of the psychiatrist is at once a breach of the duty of loyalty and the obligations of care and skill. Seeing the physician as a fiduciary and liable thus to the applicable fiduciary duties "only begins analysis," as was stated by Mr. Justice Brandeis.

It may be that different categories of fiduciaries or those that arise in different contexts may be liable for different aspects and in different degrees of the so-called fiduciary duties. This suggests a more embracing doctrine of psychiatric care.

Modern statement of this duty in the malpractice context may be seen in the recent case of *Hammonds v. Aetna Casualty and Surety Company*.[12] *Hammonds* was an action brought by a patient against the physician's malpractice insurer for allegedly inducing the physician to divulge confidential information gained through the doctor-patient relationship. The case applies to an action against a third party and thus would stand *a fortiori* in an action against the physician himself. The court spoke as follows:

> It cannot be questioned that part of a doctor's duty of total care requires him to offer his medical testimony on behalf of his patient if the patient becomes involved in litigation over the injury or illness which the doctor treated. Thus, during the

[11] Heller: "Some Comments to Lawyers on the Practice of Psychiatry, 30 *Tem. L. Q.* 401, 406, 405 (1957).

[12] 243 F. Supp. 793 (N.D. Ohio 1965).

> course of such litigation, in addition to the duty of secrecy, there arises a duty of undivided loyalty. Should a doctor breach either of these two duties, the law must afford the patient some legal recourse against such perfidy. We should not suffer a wrong without a remedy, especially when the wrong complained of involves the abuse of a fiduciary position.

In quoting then from *Alexander v. Knight*,[13] the *Hammonds* court generalized the statement of the obligation:

> We are of the opinion that members of a profession, especially the medical profession, stand in a confidential or fiduciary capacity as to their patients. They owe their patients more than just medical care for which payment is exacted; there is a duty of total care. . . .

The *Hammonds* court spoke further:

> [T]he physician-patient [relationship] is a confidential one which imposes fiduciary obligations upon the physician. As we noted above, the patient necessarily reposes a great deal of trust not only in the skill of the physician but in his discretion as well. The introduction into the relationship of this aura of trust, and the expectation of confidentiality which results therefrom, imposes the fiduciary obligations upon the doctor. As a consequence, all reported cases dealing with this point hold that the relationship of physician and patient is a fiduciary one . . . [citing cases].
>
> If the analogy expressed in the Court's earlier opinion (comparing the confidence exchanged between doctor and patient to a trust *res*) is offensive to the defendant, it comes as no surprise to the medical profession. The code of Medical Ethics itself recommends the following attitudes:
>
> "The confidences . . . should be held as a trust and should never be revealed except when imperatively required by the laws of the state."
>
> Principles of Medical Ethics of A.M.A. Ch. II, 1 (1943).
>
> Nor does the imposition of a trustee's duties upon a physician as a fiduciary fashion any new doctrine in American jurisprudence. By its very definition, the term "fiduciary relationship" imports the notion that "[I]f a wrong arises, the same remedy exists against the wrongdoer on behalf of the principal as would exist against the trustee on behalf of the *cestui que trust* . . . [citing cases]." Therefore it is readily apparent that the

[13] 197 Pa. Super. 79, 177 A.2d 142 (1962).

> legal obligations of a trustee are imposed upon any person operating in a fiduciary capacity and the same principles of law governing the behavior of a trustee are applicable to all fiduciaries.

The point made by the case is not so much that any particular facet of the physician's relationship to his patient must be governed by fiduciary obligation but that the whole and any particular facet thereof must be so structured. The relationship and the duty are therefore coextensive. The cause of action in *Hammonds* was malpractice, and the court held, therefore, that under such an allegation, a remedy for breach of trust could exist.

It is, then, this peculiarly sensitive duty of trust which gives rise to and measures the extent of the legal duty. Fixing the doctor's obligation in this fashion is not a new phenomenon. In his *Commentaries,* Blackstone[14] fixed the duty of trust as the generative touchstone of the action for malpractice.

According to Blackstone, it was for a breach of such trust that the action of malpractice would lie:

> Injuries affecting a man's *health* are where, by any unwholesome practices of another, a man sustains any apparent damage in his vigour or constitution. As . . . by the neglect or unskillful management of his physician, surgeon or apothecary. For it hath been solemnly resolved that *mala praxis* is a great misdemeanor and offense at common law, whether it be for curiosity and experiment or by neglect; because it breaks the trust which the party had placed in his physician and tends to the patient's destruction.

Doctrinally, Blackstone saw the action as arising for the breach of a contract implied in law.

It has been urged that not only is the duty of trust the aspect of the duty of the physician but that it is its touchstone. Whether this premise be adopted or instead the rather more usual statemen that duties of skill and care as well as of loyalty govern the physician, it is of certain importance that the physician be seen as practicing his profession for the patient's sole benefit. It is from the duty of loyalty that this single-minded duty of preference is derived. The fiduciary is liable for lack of the application

14 3 Blackstone: *Commentaries* 122 (Sharswood ed. 1868).

of skill and care as well as of "complete loyalty to the interests of the *cestui que trust*" to the exclusion of all selfish interests.

It has not generally been demanded that a complaint specify the duty which the umbrella of a malpractice allegation is meant to protect. But it is certain that in the context of the psychotherapeutic or analytic act, the physician must guide his patient by an interest shorn of all personal concern and by marching single-mindedly towards the patient's health. It must be understood that as in *Woods v. Brumlop*,[15] the verbal act is the subject of malpractice, so in the cause of action for damaging psychotherapeutic or analytic care, the word must be chosen and invoked with a total effort toward directing the patient toward his cure. The word or other indication of feeling must be invoked in accordance with accepted psychiatric practice as the patient's best interests dictate. It may be that medical standard is a guide to this interest, for the process of diagnosis and treatment is the process of discovering the temper of the patient's interest and subjecting that interest to the application of the medically dictated or countenanced therapy.

The psychiatrist should be expected to pursue the psychiatric or emotional well-being of his patient rather than his own emotional demands or financial or other objectives when these interests are in conflict. Applying the duty of loyalty to a given case, the consequences of the task, the risks of failure and the amount of skill necessary to minimize the dangers will determine the demands of the relationship. Thus as he chops his way in therapy or analysis, the physician must ask himself before every move What is my patient's best interest?[16] What do his needs now command? Will this hurt my patient? Am I selfishly choosing my own preferred path instead of his? It is with such a fiduciary governor that the physician should apply any given psychiatric technique. While the two aspects of fiduciary obligation may seem distinguishable in their breach, the one tending more to the intentional dereliction of duty or profiteering, as

15 71 N. Mex. 211, 377 P.2d 520 (1962).

16 *See* Hollender: "Privileged Communication and Confidentiality," Amer. Psychiatric Assn., *A Symposium on the Medico-legal Aspects of Private Psychiatric Practice* 14-15 (1965).

where his own anxiety or purse is preferred to that of the patient's, it is the former which primarily concerns us here.[17]

The nature of the psychiatric charge adds a special component to the duty of the psychiatric trustee. This is because many patients who are subjected to psychiatric care have been orally deprived of that trust which is the earliest, most enduring and possibly most important and determinative aspect of the healthy personality. It is the trust which allows a person to approach without timidity the world outside and which enables the person to proceed out of his personality shell towards behavior which involves and reacts sympathetically with other people and the total environment. So it is also that basic trust allows the healthy therapeutic identification to take place between patient and physician.

This identity of legal and medical standard makes the imposition of duty and the identification of breach the plainer. Where that basic relationship is faulted, the legal standard of breach may be invoked. It thus may be that breach of psychiatric trust may be one all-important standard and measure of breach of legal duty.

It certainly means that whenever the physician-patient emotional trust is broken in a situation where the medical profession would not consider the breach unavoidable or tolerable by medical standard, legal breach of fiduciary duty has occurred. This does not, however, mean that for a breach of duty to occur the fundamental trust relationship need be violated. The doctor need not sound at that depth for him to be in breach of duty. Damage to aspects of the total relationship may be redressable in tort.

In general, however, loyalty involves an intentional act. It is also tested in many cases not by the idea of a separation from, and dedication to, the interests or medical welfare of the patient rather than to that of the doctor, by fairness, but also—and especially in the early cases—by the absence of fraud or deceit.

There is a further issue as well. The psychiatrist is obligated

17 The trustee must not place himself in a position where his interest *may* be in conflict with his duty. Sainer: *Substantive Law of New York* 559 (1969). He must have solicitude for his own weakness.

to have that measure of control over the countertransference—his own irrational responses and anxieties—which permits the healthy development of the patient's cure. While he may not be required to have pursued a "successful" analysis himself[18] and while even the successful analysand may, like the rest of the world, be at times the victim of irrationality and anxiety,[19] the psychiatrist must minimize these reactions and think them through to the point where he is not immobilized from pursuing the patient's medical welfare. His own reactions, where, for example, he hospitalizes a patient because he unconsciously wants to get rid of him, are material to the determination of malpractice.

This is not to say that hostile unconscious motivation is actionable *per se*. Surely every action has its meaning in, and drive from, the unconscious mind. It is only that there must be a control over the unconscious on the part of the therapist that does not impede the healthy progress of the patient. The psychiatrist thus may be required to pursue a policy of caution where his own responses are in doubt and must attempt in some forms of psychotherapy and especially where tht trust of the patient is threatened, to explain and explore the issue with a patient. In this respect, the psychiatrist and his patient resemble joint venturers, each pursuing meaning and change through a virtually constant and intense quest. The ability to avoid malpractice litigation as well as a lengthy and feckless course of treatment has much to do with constant openness and mutuality of disclosure and explanation. While this is perhaps not so much the case in classic psycho-

18 *But see* Freud, "Analysis Terminable and Interminable" (1937) in Freud, *Therapy and Technique,* 233, 266-268 Rieff, ed., (1963).

> Obviously we cannot demand that the prospective analyst should be a perfect human being before he takes up analysis and that only persons of this rare and exalted perfection should enter the profession. But where and how is even the most inadequate of individuals to acquire the ideal qualifications for his work? The answer is: in his own analysis, with which he begins his profession for his future activity.

Freud goes even further:

> Every analyst ought periodically himself to enter analysis once more, at intervals of, say, five years, and without any feeling of shame in doing so.

19 Wheelis: "To Be A God," 36 *Commentary* 125 (1963). Mr. Wheelis, a psychoanalyst, describes the persistence of anxiety and melancholy in an analyst, demonstrating, for example, that some elusive "anguish" is experienced even after a third and final analysis.

analysis where the analyst's neutrality is more usual, this continued honesty maintains the trust and avoids malpractice litigation. Indeed it has been observed that "[p]roblems in malpractice involve either a breach of this [trusting] relationship by the doctor or an unusually faulty approach to the patient's problems."[20]

The most delicate problem in the relationship is to encourage closeness and identification without breeding excess and irreversible dependency. That was the problem in *Landau v. Werner,* where the failure of resolution of the problem accounted for the litigation and the decision. In his classic statement of the temptation and obligation of the analyst, Freud demonstrated how the temptation of power in the transference should not be disloyally employed:

> [T]he relation of transference brings with it two further advantages. If the patient puts the analyst in the place of his father (or mother), he is also giving him the power which his super-ego exercises over his ego, since his parents were, as we know, the origin of his super-ego. The new super-ego now has an opportunity for a sort of *after-education* of the neurotic; it can correct mistakes for which his parents were responsible in educating him. But at this point, a warning must be given against misusing this new influence. However much the analyst may be tempted to become a teacher, model and ideal for other people and to create men in his own image, he should not forget that that is not his task in the analytic relationship and indeed that he will be disloyal to his task if he allows himself to be led on by his inclinations. If he does, he will only be repeating a mistake of the parents who crushed their child's independence by their influence, and he will only be replacing the patient's earlier dependence by a new one. In all his attempts at improving and educating the patient, the analyst should respect his individuality. The amount of influence which he may ligitimately allow himself will be determined by the degree of developmental inhibition present in the patient. Some neurotics have remained so infantile that in analysis, too, they can only be treated as children.[21]

20 Heller, *op. cit. supra* note 11 at 406; *but see* Davidson, *Forensic Psychiatry* 287 (2d ed. 1965): "Many psychiatric patients are inherently litiginous [*sic.*] Some patients confuse fact with fantasy, and fantasy often leads to charges of odd behavior."

21 Freud, *An Outline of Psycho-Analysis,* p. 32 (1940) (Strachey, ed. 1969).

CONFLICT OF INTEREST: PSYCHIATRIST-PATIENT

The fiduciary by necessity has an interest in the relationship. He cannot, as with property—a segregable trust *res*[22]—segregate the *res* with which he is dealing except, perhaps, in terms of particular hypothesized causes of conduct where the patient will be acting. Thus if the patient tells him that he is attempting to purchase a house which the psychiatrist had been wanting himself to purchase, he may be under a duty to forego the purchase, but certainly at the outset he must reveal his intention and interest to the patient. (This, of course, assumes that the psychiatrist is not conducting a strict Freudian-style analysis where the psychiatrist's reactions verbally are kept to a minimum.) He thus may be liable to disclose his interest if not to give up his extratherapeutic acts. This is why fee-setting, or charging for a missed appointment is such a difficult area. The trust may, in a sense, be said to embrace every action or sphere of action which is the proper sphere of the patient's realistic concern and, under the reasoning of the doctrine of corporate opportunity, which would logically be, were the patient to know about it. If the doctor has a tip on a stock and knows the patient is buying adverse to the tip, he may be under a duty to tell him if it is in the area of the patient's problem. The message of *Landau v. Werner* in thus in terms of conflict of interest thinking, that of removing oneself when the relationship is overambiguized or the doctor has allowed his selfish love interests to intrude. There may be a suggestion of intimacy beyond what would customarily be thought proper for the fiduciary in the case.

Other consequences flow from this trust relationship. Monetary gifts or books accepted by a psychiatrist in the course of treatment may have to be returned.[23]

Since the words confided are the trust *res,* or at least their factual and perhaps their emotive content is as well, ripening sometimes into a corporate opportunity, the psychiatrist cannot tell them to a third person, for this violates the terms of the trust.

What of the duty to impart his own experiences when the pa-

[22] *See Restatement, Trusts* 2d § 170 (1959) (comment).

[23] *See Restatement, Trusts* 2d § 170 (1959).

tient would be helped by hearing them? This also is an invaluable aspect of treatment.

The duty to administer the trust is a duty of application.[24] The psychiatrist must modulate and utilize his own anger and other emotive responses in the service of the patient's treatment.

THE PSYCHIATRIST'S INTEREST AND THE COUNTERTRANSFERENCE

Aside from the variety of conscious interests which he may pursue, the psychiatrist may have some duty to control his own emotional needs, conscious as well as unconscious.[25] To be sure, he may pursure interests of his own: surely his financial interest in being compensated, his professional interest in achieving a successful treatment, and his own emotional welfare are not to be completely denied. Undoubtedly, he must maintain his emotional stability if only because without it his capacity to empathize and participate in the therapy by infusing it with his own energy might be lost. However, the interest must be followed only to the extent that it does not conflict with, but rather tends to serve, the patient's emotional well-being. If the psychiatrist hurts himself emotionally, he might imperil the patient's stability.

On the other hand, if allowances were not made for the possible psychological involvement of the psychiatrist, perhaps only an emotionally flat analyst with no emotional needs of his own would be legally protected against a malpractice action. The law does not appear to require that a psychiatrist who seeks to defend against a malpractice action have been successfully analyzed.[26] His every action need not be drive reduced and free of neurotic motive, nor need it be uniformly recognized or accepted as drive reduced by the psychiatric community. If, indeed, it were required of psychiatrists that their emotional understand-

[24] There is, however, in this personal service contract no remedy in specific performance. *Cf Restatement, Trusts* 2d § 199. (1959)

[25] *See* Greenson: "The Classic Psychoanalytical Approach" in 2 *American Handbook of Psychiatry* 1399, 1409, 1413 (Arieti, ed. 1959); Fisch, "Resistance to Change in the Psychiatric Community," 13 *Arch. Gen. Psychiat.* 359, 360-361 (1965).

[26] A failure to have undergone analysis may be the case among psychiatric residents or interns.

ing be complete in the view of the psychiatric community, there might not be enough psychiatrists available for the treatment of the mentally ill. Even the psychiatric resident—a learner who may yet lack full understanding of his own motives—must be utilized to provide therapy.[27] Psychiatry remains a scarce resource.

On the other hand, some measure of understanding of and control over the countertransference ("a transference reaction of the therapist to his patient"[28]) is prerequisite to a defense of an action in malpractice.[29] However, the extent of insight into and control over one's own motives and over the countertransference need not be complete to be legally protected. The standard of practice of the medical profession must be the guide to the case-by-case solution of this problem.

The failure to exercise such control in a given case, however, may be difficult to prove because of the limited external verifiability of a person's motives, so many of which may be unconscious. An example from the psychiatric treatment of suicidal patients

27 *See* Ungerleider: "That Most Difficult Year," 122 *Amer. J. Psychiat.* 542 (1965). As far as interns are concerned, the case law does not convincingly demonstrate that they are chargeable either with the standard of care of a student or, on the other hand, with that of a licensed professional. *See* Note, 95 *U. Pa. L. Rev.* 239 (1946). In the closest treatment of the situation, the court held for the defendant, an unlicensed dental intern, since there was no expert testimony that his practice was not in accord with the standard of the profession. Haliburton v. General Hosp. Soc'y of Connecticut, 133 Conn. 61, 48 A.2d 261 (1946). *But cf,* Owl Drug Co. v. Crandall, 52 Ariz. 322, 80 P.2d 952 (1938); Christensen v. Des Moines Still College of Osteopathy & Surgery, 248 Iowa 810, 82 N.W.2d 741 (1957); Carey v. Davis, 190 Iowa 720, 180 N.W. 889 (1921); Nickley v. Eisenberg, 206 Wis. 265, 239 N.W. 426 (1931); *see also* Shull v. Schwartz, 364 Pa. 554, 73 A.2d 402 (1950).

28 Greenson, *supra* note 25, at 1413. "Countertransference can be roughly defined as the converse of transference: the repetition of previously acquired attitudes toward the patient, such attitudes being irrational in the given situation." Cohen, "Countertransference and Anxiety," in Thompson, ed., *An Outline of Psychoanalysis* 539 (1955). "When in the patient-analyst relationship, anxiety is aroused in the analyst with the effect that communication between the two is interfered with by some alteration in the analyst's behavior (verbal or otherwise), then countertransference is present." *Id.* at 547. (Emphasis omitted.) Such a definition thus includes "all situations where the analyst was unable to be useful to the patient because of difficulties with his own responses." *Id.* at 546.

29 Landau v. Werner (C.A. Nov. 22, 1961) in *The Times* (London), Nov. 23, 1961, p. 5, col. 1.

will suffice. A psychiatrist has pointed out[30] that decisions, once made in the security of a locked ward, are now made on the outside, thus creating anxiety among psychiatrists.[31] This anxiety may be transmitted to the patient, so that the patient utilizes the suicidal defense. The physician may thus be compelled to ask himself in a given case whether his concern about the possibility of suicide derives from the patient's needs or from his own desire to be rid of the patient. In a similar vein, the psychiatrist might decide to hospitalize the patient as a way of getting rid of him. Sensing this, the patient might turn to suicide. Here the doctor's own hostility toward his patient may determine the patient's action. A suicide attempt can thus be precipitated by the psychiatrist's covert attempt to be rid of the patient by sending him to a remote institution.

Understanding the legal import of these situations requires us to make a distinction between psychoanalytic interpretation and the breach of duty. It may be difficult to prove, for example, that sending a patient to a remote hospital amounts to a breach of duty. This is not only because, unlike many who bring actions for wrongful commitment, the patient is admittedly in need of psychiatric treatment. Furthermore, proof of a hostile unconscious motive on the psychiatrist's part does not necessarily amount to a breach of duty. Nevertheless, psychoanalytic interpretation has not yet been clearly excluded from the scope of permissible expert testimony, though its comprehension and acceptance by the jury cannot be guaranteed. The question in each case should be whether the doctor has taken undue advantage of the relationship for the pursuit of personal gain; whether he has demonstrated a control of his own motives which falls below the standard of the relevant psychiatric community, not alone whether his treatment was an expression of his unconscious hostility toward the patient.

30 Address by Milton Rosenbaum, M.D., George Washington University Symposium on Suicide, October 14, 1965.

31 *Compare* Ungerleider, *supra* note 27, at 543. For a more generalized treatment of liability in cases of suicide, see Schwartz: "Civil Liability For Causing Suicide: A Synthesis of Law and Psychiatry" 24 *Vand. L. Rev.* 217 (1971); Perr: "Liability of Hospital and Psychiatrist in Suicide," 122 *Amer. J. Psychiat.* 631 (1965). *See also* Hirsh v. State, 8 N.Y.2d 125, 168 N.E.2d 372 (1960); Collins v. State, 23 App. Div. 2d 898, 258 N.Y.S.2d 938 (1965).

In deciding whether the psychiatrist should be held liable for the suicides in the examples given, the court would thus proceed on a two-step course. It would first decide whether the psychiatrist's degree of control of his own anxiety or of his hostile feelings toward the patient falls below the level of the relevant psychiatric community. It would then address itself to problems of causation.

UNDUE INFLUENCE

There is nothing new about requiring a physician to observe great care in separating the patient's interest from that of his own. It has long been recognized that the physician's fiduciary caste and his position of power transcending respect require him to abhor any opportunity to reap personal financial or other benefits at the expense of his patient. Accordingly the cases holding him liable for rewards springing from his abuse of confidence and "undue influence" over his patients describe a barrier against greedy temptation.[32] Thus a release from liability for the permanent injury resulting from having been struck by her physician's horse-driven carriage was insufficient to bar the action where the release was obtained by promises of full recovery under a promised treatment and some money.[33] Where an 84-year-old intestate had given a considerable sum of money to her physician prior to her death, evidence of her weakness of mind and complete reliance

[32] *See* Pomeroy: *Equity* § 963 (5th ed. 1941).

[33] Butler v. Gleason, 214 Mass. 248, 101 N.E. 371 (1913). Wrote the court, at p. 251-252:

> The defendant maintains, that the representation was merely an encouraging statement not intended as anything more than the expression of a hopeful expectation, which does not constitute actionable deceit. But the relation of physician to his patient is necessarily one of trust and confidence, and commercial transactions between them where fraud or undue influence is charged, are viewed by the courts with some jealousy, and are carefully scrutinized. *Woodbury v. Woodbury,* 141 Mass. 329, 331, 332. *Old Colony Trust Co. v. Bailey,* 202 Mass 283. *Dent. v. Bennett,* 4 Myl. & Cr. 269. *Allen v. Davis,* 4 DeG & Sm. 133. If he solicits and procures a conveyance to himself of the property of his patient, whether by way of gift or of purchase, the burden, where the good faith of the transaction is attacked, rests upon him to show, that the patient's confidence has not been abused, and that undue influence has not been exerted. It is not sufficient that the patient [252] knew what he was doing, but the question is how the intention was produced. *Woodbury v. Woodbury,* 141 Mass. 329. *Zeigler v. Illinois Trust and Savings Bank,* 245 Ill. 180. *Cadwallader v. West,* 48 Mod. 483. *Huguenin v. Baseley,* 14 Ves. 273. *Dent. v. Bennett,* 4 Myl. & Cr. 269. *Lyon v. Home,* L.R. 6 Eq. 655.

upon the physician in all of her most personal[34] affairs was sufficient to affirm a judgment for money had and received in the amount of 2,861 dollars by her administrator.[35]

Such cases, while not prohibitive of any special benefit being given psychiatrists as a result, for example, of special gratitude, are nevertheless highly cautionary. A trial court instruction to the jury, approved by the Massachusetts Supreme Court many years ago,[36] still provides guidance to the attitude which most courts would follow:

> When a fiduciary or confidential relation is established between a donor and a donee, a case arises for watchfulness on the part of those who have to pass on the validity of the gift, to see that this confidence has not been abused by the exercise of undue influence. The mere existence of such a confidential relation does not, as a matter of law, operate to bar the right of the beneficiary to receive such a bounty. . . . But the law views transactions of this kind between such parties with some jealousy. . . .

Psychiatry itself would likewise view the bestowal of special benefits, be they directly monetary or indirect such as corporate "insider information" as possibly overreaching on the part of therapists. As aspects of the transference relationship,[37] they might

[34] The evidence bearing on the issue of undue influence, which was deemed sufficient,

> tended to show that the donor was eighty-four years old, and was sick much of the time, weak in mind and memory, and broken down; that the gift was a large portion of the donor's estate; that the defendant who was not a relative of the donor attended her as a physician and visited her every day or twice a week; that he had charge of all her affairs and was her only advisor; that he was consulted by the donor as to employing or discharging her servants or nurses and as to her domestic affairs, and that she dressed according to his advice; that she relied upon him for direction in all her affairs; that the gift was made to the defendant without consultation with any one, and that the fact of the gift having been made was kept secret by him until after her death. It was also in evidence, that when the donor's relatives visited her, the defendant remained away.
> Woodbury v. Woodbury, 141 Mass. 329, 330-331, 5 N.E. 275, 276-277 (1886)

[35] Woodbury v. Woodbury, 141 Mass. 329, 5 N.E. 275, (1886).

[36] *Ibid.*

[37] It is striking that the catalogue of acts amounting to undue influence in the *Woodbury* case, note 35 *supra* reads like the kinds of dependency often found in, and pursued in order to establish, the transference relationship. *But see* Zipkin v. Freeman, 436 S.W.2d (Mo. 1968) (mishandling of transference). Those therapies which encourage such dependency in order to achieve healthy identification (the patient modeling himself after the therapist) would encourage many of the same acts. The difference in loyal therapy is that no personal advantage is taken of the

not only be approached more favorably as held in trust pending their interpretation, to be returned either upon request or more definitely at the time of termination, rather than being uniformly disapproved.

---

closeness. Where it is, not only disloyalty but lack of skill and care also may be established. This is because the betrayal of intimacy and confidence by a psychoanalyst or psychotherapist can break apart the whole relationship and confirm the feelings of betrayal in prior family life. Severe reactions would not be unusual.

Chapter V

The Standard of Care: Problems of Proof

It is important to note that disagreement among psychiatrists, as between witnesses for plaintiff and for defendant, pertaining to the proper treatment to be administered, does not mean that liability will obtain. As the court noted in *Taig v. State*:[1]

> The decision to release the patient from the hospital and place him on convalescent status was a medical judgment and the decision to continue him on convalescent out-patient status after February, 1955, and to discharge him in June were also matters of professional medical judgment. Although another physician might disagree as to the form and period of treatment to be followed, a liability would not occur. . . .

Deviance from a proven community standard of care must be shown. In *Daniels v. Finney*,[2] it was held insufficient to prove by expert testimony that the witness differed from the defendant in his diagnosis. It was necessary to support both a claim in malicious prosecution and malpractice for a diagnosis leading to a lunacy charge by an expert's proof that the diagnosis was negligent. The breach in the standard of care must be proven by a physician of the same school as the defendant: "[W]hat one doctor would or could do is not the test. It must be testified to unequivocably by a doctor that the diagnosis made by the defendant doctor was negligent."[3]

The standard of care is generally proven by the testimony of plaintiffs' medical experts to just such a community standard.[4]

1 19 App. Div. 2d 183, 241 N.Y.S.2d 496 (1963).
2 262 S.W.2d 431 (Tex. Civ. App. 1953).
3 262 S.W.2d at 434.
4 This requirement has not been confined to cases of malpractice. Beaumont v. Morgan, 427 F.2d 667 (1st Cir. 1970).

The reluctance of experts to so testify has been noted.[5] As one psychiatrist has observed:

> Too many physicians believe that it is unethical to testify against a colleague. If more physicians would only read the Code of Ethics of the American Medical Association—as adopted, too, by the American Psychiatric Association—they would see that a professional man is expected to speak up in the face of wrong.[6]

But the issue is not entirely a question of ethics. Time, financial deprivation, fear of reprisal and compromise of a reticence to come forth from a realm of privacy and confidence may loom among the motivations contributing to the "conspiracy of silence."[7]

These factors may have contributed to the fact in *Landau v. Werner,* for example, that the medical testimony before the court was taken as a uniform condemnation of social visits. Such uniformity may have been only an accident of proof. More likely, however, is that testimony for Dr. Werner's technique was difficult to obtain because of the added uncertainty in proving a standard of practice in the revelant psychiatric community.

When faced with behavior "whose very nature bespeaks improper treatment and malpractice," courts have not required expert testimony to establish that such behavior is wrongful. In *Hammer v. Rosen,* for example, the Court of Appeals held that it was error not to submit the issue of malpractice to the jury, even though no expert testimony to the fact had been adduced. The testimony of three witnesses that the defendant had beaten his patient on a number of occasions made out a prima facie case.[8] This rule has been elsewhere recognized in cases of psychiatric malpractice where severe assaults have resulted in physical injury to the patient.[9]

5 Note, "Malpractice and Medical Testimony," 77 *Harv. L. Rev.* 333 (1963).

6 Comments by William A. Bellamy, M.D., at the American Psychiatric Association program on "The Medico-Legal Aspects of Private Psychiatric Practice" in May, 1963, in *A Symposium on the Medico-Legal Aspects of Private Psychiatric Practice* 36 (1965): "Of course, he can speak up to the fellow physician involved, or to the Grievance Committee of the Medical Society, or to the Ethics Committee of the American Psychiatric Association."

7 Higher pay for expert witnesses may help somewhat.

8 *See,* note 10, *infra.* It virtually waived its objection on this fact.

9 Bellandi v. Park Sanitarium Assn., 214 Cal. 472, 6 P.2d 508 (1931) (death by

But the important point in *Hammer* was that the defendant chose to deny that physical beating was—as were the social visits in *Landau*—a therapeutic strategem. Said the Court of Appeals:

> In point of fact, the defendant can hardly urge that the plaintiff must call an expert to demonstrate the impropriety of the assaultive acts charged against him in view of the acknowledgement, contained in his brief in this court, that any mode of treatment which involves assaults upon the patient is fantastic.[10]

This emerges as a trial maneuver, since the defendant had several years previously written a medical work which suggested that physical slaps or other acts might be necessary in the therapy of assaultive patients:[11]

> You are frequently called upon to engage in an encounter which may require no more than that you out-glare the patient or stand your ground firmly as he assumes an angry, threatening attitude toward you, or you may actually be the victim of as much of a physical assault as the patient's strength makes possible. . . . Ordinarily interpreting the aggression neutralizes these situations. Sometimes you have to match and overcome physical violence with physical strength.

As the quotation suggests, some measure of physical restraint on the part of a psychiatrist is sometimes called for.[12] The difficulty encountered is that the publishing of a medical text does not, in and of itself, and without community adoption, necessarily make express a standard of care.

In fact there are several acts that are necessary to lend com-

---

choking employed to restrain patient); Burton v. Leftwich, 123 So.2d 766 (La. Ct. App. 1960) (assault and battery upon child patient employed to keep her still while removing sutures); Note, 77 *Harv. L. Rev.* 333, 346 n. 81 (1963). The doctrine of *res ipsa loquitur* is sometimes applied in this context. *See* Sawyer v. Jewish Chronic Disease Hosp., 234 N.Y.S.2d 372, 374 (Sup. Ct. 1962). *Hammer v. Rosen* should not be read to condemn all physical restraint, whether by straps or hand, when it is necessary to control the patient. *See generally* Annot., 89 *A.L.R.2d* 983 (1963).

10 7 N.Y.2d at 380, 165 N.E.2d at 757.

11 Rosen: *Direct Analysis* 16, 26 (1953), quoted in Katz, Goldstein and Dershowitz: *Psychoanalysis, Psychiatry and Law,* 721-722 (1967): *see* Morse: *"The Tort Liability of the Psychiatrist,"* 18 *Syracuse L. Rev.* 691 (1967), 19 *Baylor L. Rev.* 208 (1967).

12 Indeed, contrary to one of the encounter movement's preeminent suggestions, physical contact between doctor and patient or among patients in a group therapy is severely discouraged.

munity acceptance and the necessary adoption to medical writing. It is not that a standard may not be recognized, adopted, taught, and utilized without having been reduced to writing. It is only more likely that a community standard has been written about and as a writing, be easier to be referred to in court. Thus, for example, we may differentiate between a paper,[13] a published writing, a widely used text and a report of,[14] or canon of standards to be applied by, a professional body. When there is a canon of the last variety, which is only sometimes the case, proof by expert testimony may not be necessary. Thus, in *Stone v. Proctor*,[15] where electroshock treatments of increased intensity and duration were continued and no x-ray administered despite the patient's complaint of pain, the court held it negligent so to fail to prescribe x-rays of the patient and thus to aggravate a thoracic vertebral compression fracture. It was held, in fixing the standard of care, that proof of the plaintiff's case by setting forth the stand-

13 Which, if it is insufficiently documented may be insufficient to establish a community standard. Thus, in *Saron v. State,* 24 App. Div.2d 771, 263 N.Y.S.2d 591 (1965), it was held that the Court of Claims properly declined to find, upon the record before it, that the administering of the so-called Compound 100 (isonicotinic acid hydrazine) constituted negligence on the part of physicians in a State hospital where claimant's intestate was a voluntary patient upon a diagnosis of schizophrenia. Wrote the court:

> Indeed, the testimony as to the allegedly then-known harmful side effects of this medication were equivocal at best and the doctor's [claimant's medical witness'] opinion that the prescription of the drug was contrary to accepted medical practice at the time, because the side effects were known in 1952, seems to rest on an article published in England in November of that year, which apparently reported but a single case; and his conclusion that the dosage was excessive seems to have been derived from a report or reports issued subsequent to decedent's death. Further, he conceded that the brain damage "could . . . have occurred other than with the use of Compound 100," that "it could have occurred from the abnormal metabolic state, namely, the diabetes."

Id. at 771-772, 263 N.Y.S.2d at 592-593.

14 *See e.g.* American Psychiatric Association, Task Force Report, *Encounter Groups and Psychiatry* (1970):

> Manifestly, the findings, opinions and conclusions of Task Force Reports do not necessarily represent the views of the officer [sic], trustees, or all members of the Association. Each report, however, does represent the thoughtful judgment and consensus of the task force of experts who formulated it and it is considered by the Trustees a useful and substantive contribution to the ongoing analysis and evaluation of problems, programs, issues, and practices in a given area of concern.

Waggoner, *id.* at 1.

15 259 N.C. 633, 131 S.E.2d 297 (1963).

ards of the American Psychiatric Association made it unnecessary to prove its case by expert testimony.[16] The defendant's acknowledgment of the authenticity of the Association's standards and their applicability to the Winston-Salem area was sufficient to warrant their admission in evidence.[17] Thus even such standards were open to dispute. Furthermore, there are different levels of adoption of standards by different internal APA groups as well as the requirement of adoption or applicability to the particular geographical area of practice.

Unforunately, the guidance which such standards can contribute is not found in all areas of psychiatric practice and especially in the area of psychoanalysis and psychotherapy.

PROOF OF THE STANDARD OF CARE; DEVIANCE THEREFROM; PROXIMATE CAUSE AND INJURY

The holdings in *Hammer v. Rosen* and in *Bellandi v. Park Sanitorium Assn.*[18] state the apparently common rule, that, as stated by Professor Curran,[19] and unlike other types of cases,

> [u]nder the present law a plaintiff cannot avoid a directed verdict for the defendant physician unless he produced expert medical testimony in regard to the applicable standard of medical practice except in rare cases of *res ipsa loquitur* or where common lay knowledge is enough to judge the defendant's conduct as malpractice.[20]

16 These were the "standards for electroshock treatment" prepared by the APA's Committee on Therapy and approved by the Association's Council. They were considered non-controversial and reflecting the consensus of those who practice such therapy. They were also the same as those which a practicing doctor could observe in his practice in that area. *Ibid.*

17 259 N.C. 633, 131 S.E.2d 297.

18 214 Cal. 472, 6 P.2d 508 (1931). In *Bellandi,* the decedent had been choked by the application of a tourniquet to his neck in an attempt to calm him. There was contemporaneous application of practically a whole can full of ether. The court refused to reverse a jury verdict of 15,000 dollars for either etherizing or choking him to death. Cf. Phillip v. United States Lines Company, 240 F. Supp. 992 (E.D. Pa. 1965).

19 Curran: *Law and Medicine* 742 (1960). Affirmative testimony of experts has recently been required in *Dimitrijevic v. Chicago Wesley Memorial Hospital,* 92 Ill. App. 2d 251, 236 N.E.2d 309 (1968). *See,* Annot., 99 *A.L.R.2d* 599 (1969); *see, generally,* 2 Harper and James: *Torts,* 963, 968 (1956).

20 Such lay knowledge is invoked by grossly apparent negligence. 2 Harper and James: *Torts* 963, 968 (1956); Prosser: *Torts,* 167 (3rd. ed. 1964).

The expert "must say that the defendant's treatment deviated from any of the methods of treatment approved by the standard of the profession in that community."[21] Once expert testimony has been presented as required, courts "permit the jury to resolve conflicts of opinion among expert witnesses and come to their own conclusions about the proper standard of conduct."[22] Resort to this rule in *Hammer v. Rosen* seems to have been a good way of avoiding the deeper question of the efficacy or legal regularity of a treatment mode whose status had perhaps not yet been fully realized, explored or accepted by the medical community.[23] It is indeed not clear that the case should have been handled on this basis, rather than on a more adequate exploration of the facts. It is the fallacy of many or almost any psychotherapeutic or analytic malpractice action that the patient and physician may have been alone with each other when the alleged harmful activity took place, so that there is no adequate proof of the event aside from the word of an often wealthy physician[24] against that of a sad and often helpless victim of an illness which even the ablest psychiatrist is sometimes helpless to remedy.[25]

EVIDENCE OF PROXIMATE CAUSE: PROBLEMS OF PROOF: "HOW DO YOU PROVE YOUR PSYCHIATRIST INJURED YOU?"

Another phase of the problem of proof is the disparity in acumen of perception or memory between the psychiatrist and the mentally ill patient . The former is presumably not the victim of a perceptive disorder, as many psychiatric patients are likely to be. The transference itself breeds the misapplication of feelings

21 *Id.* at 969.

22 *Ibid.*

23 The opinion was criticized in Morse, "The Tort Liability of the Psychiatrist," 18 *Syracuse L. Rev.* 19 *Baylor L. Rev.* 208 (1967).

24 *Cf.* e.g. Gasperini v. Manginelli, 196 Misc. 547, 92 N.Y.S.2d 575 (Sup. Ct. 1949) for expression of this attitude.

25 *Cf.* Louisell and Williams: *Trial of Medical Malpractice Cases* § 2.16 p. 51 (1970); "Proof or disproof of alleged details of a transaction between a psychiatrist and a patient who actually requires psychiatric treatment perhaps constitutes one of the most difficult problems in medico-legal affairs."

to the therapist. Anger may be high and imaginings rampant. This would be especially true with the hospitalized psychotic. This is why a pattern of physical abuse as in *Hammer* is so much easier to establish than the negligent use of words with no third parties present to verify what, in fact, took place.

But neither sympathy for the patient nor exalting the position of the psychiatrist should determine the matter. As the New York Court of Appeals stated in *Carpenter v. Blake:*[26]

> The defendant swears that when he set the arm he extended, flexed, and rotated it, where he set the joint, to ascertain whether the bones were in the right place and that he was satisfied that they were. The plaintiff denies that this was done. It is not questioned but this was the proper and correct treatment for such a case, and although it is quite probable that the defendant was in a better condition to know and to remember what he did than the plaintiff, who was nervous and afflicted with pain, yet it was for the jury to say where the truth lay, in reference to this branch of the case. To contend that the testimony of the attending surgeons is entirely controlling is to ignore well-settled principles, which are applicable to trials of issues of fact before a jury.[27]

And thus, as exposed in *Landau v. Werner,*[28] the legal issue may often form a helpful method of resolving the conflict in a way that allows full recompense to the victim, without either ruining the psychiatrist's practice or creating a tangled legal decision which no lawyer can easily unravel. Therefore, it may be helpful to explore the other ways of handling these conflicts, such as medical boards with legal referees. Such methods might inhibit open and successful interview. Even more difficult might be the issues of proof raised by group therapy or allied reality or actuality therapies where many are present, where issues of group loyalty and loyalty to the therapist are raised and where the legal trial may be only a neurotic ploy in the eyes of the group's plaintiff and defendant.

26 75 N.Y. 12, 18 (1878).

27 *Ibid.*

28 (C.A. Nov. 22, 1961) in *The Times* (London) Nov. 23, 1961, p. 5, col. 1.

On the whole, *Hammer v. Rosen* may be an adequate solution of the problem, at least, of an advanced or physically somewhat brutal or innovative mode of therapy.[29] Its setting in a clinical office rather than a hospital where immediate restraint rather than therapeutic objective is the immediate cause of the physical impact, makes neither *Burton v. Leftwich*[30] nor *Bellandi v. Park Sanitarium Assn.*[31] entirely applicable, and the therapeutic objective may have been perceived by the judge, despite his diatribe, and have been set to one side in order to accomplish a benchmark of decency, quiet public alarm, and warn psychiatrists, cohere with other doctrines of the law, and achieve a beneficial result in a rather hard case. The anxiety within the psychiatric community itself on the issue of hitting a patient may have been substantial, and the court may have performed beneficially the function of cauterizing conduct or bringing it to a head and slightly intruding itself into a public activity in order to gently mention its interest in public safety, sound recompense, and clear statement of fact.

Another issue is that of the recognition of harm caused where there has been no physical impact, but only emotional harm, such as the traditional situation where fright or chagrin has been experienced. *Hammer v. Rosen* may have been an attempt to assert jurisdiction over psychiatrists and their treatments before *Ferrara v. Galluchio*[32] made the impact rule's disappearance eventual. It demonstrates the shift from the phrase that "[m]ental pain or anxiety the law cannot value, and does not pretend to redress, when the unlawful act complained of causes that alone,"[33] to the realization that "the courts have already given extensive protection to feelings and emotions. . . . No longer is it even approximately true that the law does not pretend to redress mental pain and anguish 'when the unlawful act complained of causes that alone'."[34]

29 *But cf.* Morse, note 23 *supra,* who considered Dr. Rosen's treatment mode recognized by virtue of publication of his methods.

30 123 So. 2d 766 (La. Ct. App. 1960).

31 214 Cal. 472, 6 P.2d 508 (1931).

32 5 N.Y.2d 16, 152 N.E.2d 249 (1958).

33 Lynch v. Knight, 9 H.L. Cas. 577, 598 (1861) sp. quoted in Magruder: "Mental and Emotional Disturbance in the Law of Torts," 49 *Harv. L. Rev.* 1033 (1936).

34 Magruder, *supra* note 33, at 1067.

Thus the suggestion in the isolated New York case of *Kraus v. Spielberg*[35] that fright and resulting psychic injury brought on by words alone are not compensable is probably to be given limited attention.

The interesting thing about the psychiatric malpractice cases is that they evidence a situation where the harm caused is in the mode of the treatment itself or of the illness being treated and is thus like the breaking of or hindering of the curing of an elbow while it is being treated. It differs, then, in primary subject matter here from that of the *Hammer* injury, though that case showed an injury during the therapy, for the therapeutic act or tactic was injurious and a harm-causing device, though the harm complained of was not in the emotional realm. It was a direct as opposed to a more circuitous *Palsgraf*[36] chain of causation. These distinctions may be important for types of result in different cases. It may also be important to distinguish alleging an entire strategy as an injury or merely one tactic or therapeutic act. There neither would, nor should be, any necessary requirement that the one rather than the other should be the legal requirement for a cause of action, though it may be that the amount of injury or harm caused in either must be inversely proportionate to the particular scope of injury or harm. There are thus possible other harms such as direct financial loss, human loss as of friends, or family, or job loss; but the coin of the injury or harm is of less importance here than is the fact or variety of therapeutic acts or acts which come within the scope of the therapy for this purpose of alleging and proving a psychiatric malpractice action. Their scope is governed by the usual concepts of proximate cause, injury, harm and damage, and less by untraditional means, though the recognition of what the technique is, and the proof of it to the jury and to the judge may be a more difficult thing.

[35] 37 Misc. 2d 519, 236 N.Y.S.2d 143 (Sup. Ct. 1962) (erroneous information to a patient that she had tuberculosis germs in her stomach). The court wrote: "No case has been brought to my attention which holds a doctor liable for causing fright and a psychic injury brought on by a statement in the course of his diagnosis or treatment." *Id.* at 520-521, 236 N.Y.S. 2d at 145.

[36] Palsgraf v. Long Island R.R., 248 N.Y. 339, 162 N.E. 99 (1928).

VARIETIES OF INJURY

There are various complaints of harm caused in relation to, or after, psychiatric acts of diagnosis, treatment or therapy. These may include physical complaints such as fracture, death, beating or compensation neuroses such as hives, acne, upset stomach. They may include emotional injuries such as depression, fatigue, elation, schizophrenia, psychoses all caused directly or by the intervention of third parties. Or they may obtain in the external world and include also or instead loss of money,[37] job, consortium, break-up of an engagement,[38] divorce, incarceration in a mental hospital, being called mentally ill publicly or making a third person aware of psychiatric illness or other intimacies about one's life or comprise simple lack of amelioration[39] by therapy. Such complaints are very real and may be considered harm, though perhaps be no worse than, or a return to, prior states, happening thus to the chronic job loser, divorcer, physically injured (though questionable as we characteristically consider such injury segregable[40]) or depressed person.

Our question is, first, then, whether these injuries can be caused by psychiatrists in their professional roles and, second, whether they can be attributed to avoidable mistakes by these doctors in their professional acts. Their attribution may only initiate a lawsuit. Recovering damages for these acts demands that a complexity of legal standards must be met. There must be a legal duty of skill, care and loyalty which is established by a school of practice adhered to by the defending psychiatrist, which standard together with proof that the act or acts or failure to act was beneath the standard of that school in a degree which amounts to negligence. Both must be proved by expert testimony except in the rare cases where the injury could not have happened without negligence *(res ipsa loquitur)* or where the injury is so easily classified as negligent by the general public that the jury or a judge can determine it is negligent without the benefit of expert

37 *See* Zaremba v. Woods, 17 Cal. App. 2d 309, 61 P.2d 976 (1936) (testamentary disposition obtained by undue influence).

38 Harriott v. Plimpton, 166 Mass. 585, 44 N.E. 996 (1896).

39 *See* Hammer v. Rosen, 7 N.Y.2d 376, 165 N.E.2d 756. (1960).

40 Accident proneness could be an injury caused by a psychiatrist.

testimony. Proximately caused damage is not enough. We are therefore thrust upon a study of negligence in the therapies: to what the profession itself would consider—through the testimony of expert witnesses—a breach of that school's standard of clinical behavior: skill, care and loyalty.

Psychiatric schools may hesitate at such appraisals because they are dealing with an inexact science where trial and error or experimentation is the method of care itself. Such stopgaps as a failure to have been analyzed on the part of the therapist may be introduced as negligence *per se*.[41] This is to be disfavored according to other experts or schools. Licensing laws have not, in general, answered this problem. There is also a self-protective idea among psychiatric schools which fosters comparison with the aspects of a sect[42] constantly reaching for its own self-respect or identity with threats, especially from those aspects of it who push away from the medical and more towards the nonmedical and even evangelical. Thus we may see in the new group therapies—the encounter groups and sensitivity training sessions—aspects of an Awakening, with little verification of ideology and treatment available. In these sessions, leaders sometimes fly from city to city like the Bal Shem Tov of Chasidic Judaism, meeting their subjects only briefly and perhaps haphazardly.

Then there is the problem of dimension of injury. Mistakes are made every day in every treatment, only some of which, or the chronicity or depth of only some of which may be classified as so sustained or serious that they may be considered breaches of duty in psychiatry or actionable in law. Not every mistake is the proper basis for legal action.

Thus the rule is generally stated, as in the law of corporations where the business judgment rule was for a long time given wide scope,[43] that negligence—or breach of the duties of skill and care —may not be presumed from the fact of mistaken judgment. Thus in *Williams v. LeBar*,[44] defendant physicians had been sued for signing a certificate of plaintiff's insanity without having made a

41 *See* Jaspers: *The Nature of Psychotherapy* 37-41 (Phoenix ed. 1965).

42 *Id.* at 36.

43 Scope to the rule has been narrowed as the duty of loyalty has spread its wings.

44 141 Pa. 149, 21 Atl. 525 (1891) (per curiam).

careful examination. An examination nevertheless had been made, said the court, and the burden of showing negligence was upon the plaintiff. Even though the defendants had been mistaken and the plaintiff was found not to have been insane at the time of the examination,[45] the court ruled that:

> . . . no presumption of negligence arose from the mere fact that the defendants were mistaken as to the fact of insanity.
>
> The most the case discloses is an error of judgment, to which the most careful and skillful physician is liable in a mysterious disease like insanity.[46]

PROOF OF INJURY AND PROXIMATE CAUSE

Even where there has been some act of negligence by the psychiatrist, perhaps most significantly where he has breached his duty to the patient, the psychiatrist will not be held responsible for a subsequent injury which is not the proximate cause of his breach.[47] In short, the injury must be within the risk exposed by the breach, and the person who is injured must be among the group protected by the duty. Sometimes, however, patients who have begun psychotherapy, after having established a pattern of neurotic symptoms, experience psychotic episodes while in treatment. It must be understood that such incidents may be unavoidable in the course of therapeutic probing. However, what is peculiar in this situation is that a suit instituted after such an incident may fix liability upon the downside of a curve before

45 Generally the incarceration should be close in time to the examination, for recovery (especially with the use of tranquilizers) from an incarcerable state may be quite rapid. This is often required by the applicable statute.

46 141 Pa. 149, 21 Atl. 525.

47 Eisele v. Malone, 2 App. Div. 2d 550, 157 N.Y.S.2d 155 (1957). Plaintiff alleged negligence in the psychiatrist's continued use of shock therapy after symptoms of spinal fracture appeared. The claim was made, *inter alia,* that the hospital was negligent in failing to provide adequate x-ray facilities, and it was alleged that such an examination was essential since it would have revealed the fracture and avoided further injury. It was held that the verdict was invulnerable on this issue but that the proof did not sustain the jury's conclusion that the absence of x-ray facilities was, as it had to be, "directly related to and causative of plaintiff's condition." There was no proof that, as the jury clearly believed, the doctor would have ordered x-rays for plaintiff if such facilities had been available; *See also* Tissinger v. Wooley, 50 S.E.2d 122 (1948).

its future path upward has had a chance to emerge. The difficulty of proving injury in such a case is, in part, due to insufficient knowledge of the course of the illness. Thus the tendency in some instances to attribute failure of improvement to a breach of duty on the part of the psychiatrist may be a dangerous one.[48]

Only under rare circumstances does a psychiatrist give, and may he therefore be held to, an assurance of cure. What he engages to do ordinarily is to pursue a cure by the methods of his profession. This has been recognized by courts dealing with psy-

[48] *See* Hammer v. Rosen, 7 App. Div. 2d at 217, 181 N.Y.S.2d at 806 (1959) (dissent), *modified*, 7 N.Y.2d 376, 165 N.E.2d 756 (1960). In the dissenting opinion in the Appellate Division (with which the Court of Appeals agreed), Judge McNally observed:

> It is conceded that at the conclusion of defendant's treatment between 1948 and 1955, involving expenditures of over $55,000, the condition of the patient plaintiff had not improved. The lack of improvement despite the time lapse establishes regression rather than stabilization of her condition.

Implicit in this statement is the attitude that the injury was the lack of improvement itself.

But see Landau v. Werner (C.A. Nov. 22, 1961) in *The Times* (London), Nov. 23, 1961, p. 5, col. 1. Lord Justice Sellers stated the question as whether Dr. Werner was negligent, and if so, whether he caused a "further breakdown" in the health of Miss Landau. This statement nullifies any question raised elsewhere in the opinion as to the liability for return to her former condition. The question is a complicated one. Is the psychiatrist liable only for the declines which bring the patient below the pretherapy level of his condition? There may be a point at which a gain realized in the therapy has taken residence in the patient's personality and exists there aside from a level of substantial dependence upon the psychiatrist. The difference is between a tenancy at will and a freehold held by the psychiatrist in the patient's personality or particular defense mechanism. In between are a range of levels of dependence whose identification as "substantial" must be the product of case-by-case evaluation. Surely the psychiatrist cannot escape the consequences of malpractice which causes a decline from ego development (dependent upon identification) to its pretherapy level. On the other hand, the gains which depend upon close therapeutic support may not have been won to substantial freedom from the psychiatrist, so that their loss is understandable as having been wrested from the patient. So, likewise, are those "technical corrections" which are experiential declines from overextended positions in the development of the personality during therapy. Thus might a depressed patient become psychotic for two hours in the process of assimilating new levels of independence and ego strength. In such cases, as in cases of somewhat longer psychotic breaks which occur when emotionally laden areas are therapeutically explored, the psychiatrist ought not to be held to answer in damages.

In this connection, it has been suggested that the level of preexisting condition and the possibilities for cure determine the base line for the assessment of damages and that both involve questions for expert determination. *See* Bellandi v. Park Sanitarium Ass'n, 214 Cal. 472, 480-81, 6 P.2d 508, 512 (1931).

chiatric treatment,[49] but there has been a concomitant tendency to consider sympathetically arguments based upon the disparity between lengthy and costly treatment and failure of improvement. At some point, perhaps, there may be a duty upon a psychiatrist whose continued application has borne no visible fruit to abandon the case or to seek consultation.[50] However, only in one case, and there where the patient had "fallen in love" with the doctor, was termination of treatment considered the duty of the psychiatrist.[51] To the extent that recognition of such a duty motivates the tendency to give mere failure of improvement the weight of injury, it ought to be made explicit in the cases. To the extent that sensitivity to the disparity between fee and result is the underlying factor, the tendency is to be criticized. Proof of maintenance of condition where decline is a real possibility presents a probable line of defense. To sustain a cause of action for malpractice, there

[49] Johnston v. Rodis, 251 F.2d 917 (D.C. Cir. 1958).

> Doubtless a physician's statement that he would cure a disease could seldom if ever be regarded as a warranty. But that is not this case. The statement attributed to the defendant, that shock treatments are "perfectly safe," contains less of prediction and more of present fact. We think this statement, if the defendant made it and did not qualify it in any way, might properly be found to be a warranty.

Id. at 918. *Accord,* Howe v. New York, 33 Misc. 2d 147, 153, 226 N.Y.S.2d 933, 939 (Ct. Cl. 1962) (by implication); Hammer v. Rosen, *supra* note 48; Landau v. Werner, *supra* note 48 (by implication).

[50] In *Landau v. Werner* the Court of Appeal enunciated a duty to abandon the therapy in terms that reach broadly through the concept of duty to encompass a duty of consultation. At the moment when the patient had "fallen in love" with the psychiatrist, the court demanded Dr. Werner's withdrawal: "It seemed now that the most prudent thing for Dr. Werner to have done was to refer Miss Landau back to her own doctor and advise that the treatment was not completed and should be resumed with someone else." (C.A. Nov. 22, 1961) in *The Times* (London), Nov. 23, 1961, p. 5, col. 1.

[51] Landau v. Werner, *supra* note 50. A holding which appears on its face to be contrary to *Landau* is *Gasperini v. Manginelli,* 196 Misc. 547, 92 N.Y.S.2d 575 (Sup. Ct. 1949). In that case it was held that allegations of a defendant psychiatrist's failure to consult another psychiatrist before commencing treatment did not state a cause of action for malpractice: "Defendant was himself a psychiatrist who had been called in by the family physician. It is understandable that he did not see the need for a consulting psychiatrist." *Id.* at 550, 92 N.Y.S.2d at 578. The decision is limited to the naked requirement of employing a consulting psychiatrist at the outset of therapy and would probably not govern a state of facts where long-continued therapy had borne no apparent results. Uncertainty of result, of condition or of completed treatment may raise a duty on the part of a psychiatrist to consult.

must be proof that improvement, of which there was a substantial likelihood, was prevented by the psychiatrist's breach of duty.

On the other hand, there need be no proof of the effect of a tortious act on the course of treatment itself where there is proof of independent injury from which pain and suffering flow as natural consequences. Thus, the New York Court of Appeals held in *Hammer v. Rosen* that since "damages recoverable in malpractice are for personal injuries, including the pain and suffering which flow from the tortious act," proof of bruises will sustain a jury's finding that acts of assault have caused plaintiff pain and suffering.[52]

DAMAGES

This raises an important point about any injury dealt a psychiatric patient. In the myraid of psychiatric judgments, not every palpable decline in health is actionable. Perhaps only a congeries of setbacks or the kind of serious reaction which makes further improvement more difficult and costly is or should be the occasion for successful legal recompense. There are declines of even a psychotic nature which will not and should not be compensated for, since they may be unavoidable pitfalls in working through the tangled terrain of one's mental complexion. Research in the traditional therapies as in the encounter therapy may be sparse and the unavoidable concomitants of many treatments may be psychiatric ups and downs multiplied by intensity when compared to the usual struggles of living. Thus temporary psychosis should be separated from chronic schizophrenia in the phenomena being advanced as injury. Similarly, while some psychiatrists may interpret every act of living as being a result of the psychiatrist-patient interaction, car accidents, job or marital failures and even suicide may be difficult of causal link to acts in the therapy, or at least until more ample evidence makes the psychopathology of everyday life of more universal acceptance.

But these dynamic moments of flush or of depression are usual in psychiatric treatment and must be gauged and administered to if truly careful therapy is to take place. They surely must be

[52] 7 N.Y.2d at 378, 165 N.E.2d at 758, 198 N.Y.S.2d at 67-68.

measured in deciding what treatment direction to take or in deciding if a wrong has been committed. Thus in the only extensive judicial evaluation of a course of psychoanalysis or psychotherapy, the Queens Bench decided that the introduction of a course of social visits to a patient who had, as the predominant aspect of her transference, "fallen deeply in love with her analyst," was professional negligence (malpractice). That court's evaluation of the psychiatric or treatment moment is to be admired, even though other aspects of the judicial thought process may have left serious questions unanswered.

PROOF OF INJURY: PHYSICAL INVASION

In *Hammer v. Rosen* over the course of seven years of treatment, the patient's early improvement did not remain permanent, a result which the lower court saw as of "complex causation." At its conclusion, in 1955, after expenditures of 55,000 dollars, the child and her father instituted suit, she for malpractice, the father for breach of contract and for fraud. The trial court dismissed the malpractice and fraud causes, and allowed the jury to return a verdict for defendant on the contract cause. It was *held* error by the Court of Appeals not to submit the count charging malpractice to the jury: that the testimony of three witnesses indicating that Dr. Rosen had beaten Miss Hammer on a number of occasions made out a *prima facie* case of malpractice, for which no supportive expert testimony was required. Said the court: "[T]he very nature of the acts complained of bespeaks improper treatment and malpractice." It placed the burden of proof upon the defendant to justify the acts as proper treatment, but Dr. Rosen's brief acknowledged that such a mode of treatment was "fantastic."

Hammer v. Rosen stands for the principle that where the very nature of the acts complained of bespeaks improper treatment and malpractice, plaintiff need not adduce expert testimony to reach the jury. Here, testimony given by three of plaintiff's witnesses indicating that the doctor had beaten the girl on three occasions made out the *prima facie* case. Little guidance to the implementation of the rule is given, however, for the defendant was virtually estopped to call for experts from the plaintiff by his acknowledgment in his brief that any mode of treatment which involves assaults upon the patient is "fantastic." There is no suggestion that the rule would reach to allow plaintiff to get to a jury upon a mere *res ipsa loquitur* showing, but the case does locate a point at which judicial deference to psychiatric judgment, as with psychiatric innovation, has an end.

Where the abuse is physical, where the psychiatrist himself abandons clinical defense of his therapy, or at least positively deprecates it as such, *Hammer v. Rosen* is difficult to question. Nevertheless, there is a point at which the factors, difficult of judicial reexamination, which play their part in many less palpable therapeutic judgments, must be considered. There must be a guide to what acts themselves bespeak improper treatment, and that guide is apparently the general judicial sense, a sense which sees physical invasion, at least, as *per se* improper.

The holding in *Hammer v. Rosen* seems to have some precedent. In *Bellandi v. Park Sanitarium Ass'n,*[53] the decedent was admitted to a sanitarium the night before he was to have returned to Italy after seventeen years to visit his mother. Upon breaking out of a "strong room" and grabbing a nurse who was leaving him, he was set upon by a doctor and several nurses, was subjected to a tourniquet: toweling drawn tight about the neck, and the free use of ether. The patient died, and in this action for wrongful death, testimony was produced to support the plaintiff's contention that he had been etherized or choked to death. Said the court:

> If the jury accepted the testimony of those who appeared for the respondent and described the treatment to which the decedent was subjected, we need not go into the question as to whether the attending physician used the degree of skill ordinarily possessed by reputable physicians engaged in the practice of a special branch of science in the locality where the treatment was administered, for the reason that scientific knowledge is not essential for the determination of an obvious fact.

The lack of need for expert testimony on this issue of whether the death-causing restraint was proper practice in the community must be contrasted to the court's treatment of the prognostication

[53] 214 Cal. 472, 6 P.2d 508 (1931).

of the victim's condition, the kind of judgment prerequisite to the action of Dr. Werner:

> The probability that the deceased's condition was no more than temporary and that the prognosis was reasonably favorable for a complete restoration to health is a question which must be submitted to medical skill, and its answer on matters which are beyond the ken of the layman furnishes a basis upon which courts of law may predicate a judgment.

It is not to be understood, however, that these courts are positing a *res ipsa loquitur* standard of proof. In both cases, the acting agent, the cause of the injury, is not left to inference. There is direct testimony to the assaults by each doctor. What is left out is only the proof of experts to the standard of care, and it is left out because a pervasive community standard of correct medical behavior has been offended: "[T]he very nature of the acts complained of bespeaks improper treatment and malpractice." "[S]cientific knowledge is not essential for the determination of an obvious fact."

All of the cases may be grouped in terms of types of injury, and in that way *Hammer v. Rosen* is very typical. It was, after all, nothing new to give redress to physical bruises. *Powell v. Risser* and *Bellandi v. Park Sanitarium,* to name only two cases, dealt with just such injuries. Such cases present strong urgency and are prone to be in plaintiff's behalf. They are classic situations for the intrusion of the governing words of courts. Fractures and physical enclosure in mental institutions had also been familiar types of redress situations for courts. But more technical violations—the verbal, accusations, identifications as "lunatics"—these laid the true groundwork, for the verbal abuse or rather the verbally conceived damage, without the direct connotation or quality of abuse, was the cornerstone for the new cases.

Hammer v. Rosen presents a very comfortable situation for the court. There is beating of a helpless person without attempt to do more than deny the beatings. All idea that the abuse would be considered a therapeutic tool was abandoned probably because of a tactical judgment that the therapy might fall with its adjudication and the thought that the therapeutic methodology and freedom could be preserved if the case was tried to a jury on the grounds of denial of the primary allegations of the complaint. But there is much to be said for defendant in the case. Though the particular case was potentially disastrous for the defending physician, it may be that in depression, some controlled physical intrusion may be ameliorative by serving to objectify the source of anger and thus to pierce the wall of a very sick person. Next to the prefontal lobotomy, such incidental bruising may be almost gentle.

But while the *Hammer* case was not fought out on grounds of rectitude of a therapeutic endeavor but rather on a question of fact, the case left unclear the grounds of therapy in psychiatric cases. It seemed to say to the profession that no matter how young and innovative was the profession, and no matter how much in need of experiment and innovation, there were, nevertheless, strict ground rules, and when it came to bruising a patient not in an effort to quiet him,[54] the psychiatrist had better take heed for to think that physical beating of a patient was a *bona fide* therapeutic task was preposterous. The case had other matters as well. The judicial message may have been simply that psychotherapy was at last subjected to being governed in malpractice. For except for a less direct assault upon the citadel of medical privacy in *Rosenfeld v. Coleman*,[55] this was the first case of controlling the psychotherapeutic mode.

Its holding, dealing with the observation that the very act denotes malpractice to the layman and as such need not be proven by expert testimony, is probably sound on this point and breathes in the meaning that the standards of the profession will, in appropriate cases, be asked to conform to the rules of behavior in the community and in the court. There are some things that a psychiatrist must not do in his surgery. Then along came *Landau v. Werner* and told us that there are some things a psychiatrist may not do outside his surgery. Both cases presented legal restraint

[54] *Cf.* Burton v. Leftwich, 123 So.2d 766 (La. Ct. App. 1960), where a dentist quieted a child patient by ancillary physical restraint in the service of the therapy, though not the therapy itself and though still within the circle of doctor-patient interaction and subject to fiduciary duty.

[55] 19 Pa. D. & C. 2d 635, 35 North Co. R. 206 (C.P. Northampton County Ct. 1959). Curiously, the three cases on psychotherapeutic malpractice occurred between 1959 and 1961. But they apparently have left scant progeny in the appellate cases, though there is indication that there has been a series of lower court cases.

to the psychiatric practitioner. In *Landau,* it was the fiduciary acting almost disloyally by apparent attempt to reap personal satisfaction from the beneficiary of the fiduciary relationship.

Actually neither case was startling in doctrinal terms but they suggest that there is still hesitancy about bringing the ordinary variety of abuse in psychiatric care into the courtroom.

SOME CRITICAL COMMENTS ON THE CASES: GUIDEPOSTS FOR THE PSYCHIATRIST

For the very reason that the court is not very explicit about its standard in *Hammer v. Rosen,* the case must be taken with care. It would probably be an injustice, for example, to read the opinion as ruling that mere physical touching bespeaks improper treatment and malpractice. Sustained beating, with no purported redemptive force was at issue. *Hammer* does not, for example, attempt to proscribe the reassuring clasp, or holding the hand of the frightened nor, perhaps, the spanking of a naughty child.[56] Such behavior is acceptable in ordinary relationships, not, like the beating in *Hammer,* itself the subject of civil or criminal remedy. While *Hammer* did not rest upon the independently actionable nature of the injury, it may be read more understandingly in such a light. It is a beam which plays over *Landau v. Werner* as well: the suggestion that there is not psychiatric license to transgress boundaries of psychic as of physical intrusion upon the patient. Had the Court of Appeals rested its case upon the suggestion of adultery that was raised in *Landau v. Werner,* there might be some support to reading *Hammer v. Rosen* as establishing its guideline in other than criminal or tortious behavior.

This is not to say that psychiatric practice is not subject to its limits by the criminal order. It is, however, to suggest that mere violation of a criminal statute will not establish psychiatric malpractice and that while there is criminal behavior which, like the run of the *malum in se* offenses, probably "bespeaks improper treatment and malpractice," the tests normally applied to equating violation of a criminal statute with tortious behavior will be

[56] *See* Burton v. Leftwich, 123 So.2d 766 (La. Ct. App. 1960) (assault and battery upon child patient employed to keep her still while removing sutures).

followed. This, at least, is the suggestion in *Rosenfeld v. Coleman*[57] where it was *held* that since the purpose of the Antinarcotics Act was to prevent prescriptions for drug addiction as such, and where defendant psychiatrist had done so to the proximate cause of plaintiff's becoming a drug addict, there was sufficient evidence of negligence to grant plaintiff's motion to strike a nonsuit to his case.

Under *Rosenfeld v. Coleman,* a psychiatrist having sexual intercourse with at least an underage patient is not only guilty of statutory rape[58] but probably also liable in tort for malpractice. In *People v. Bernstein,*[59] a sixteen-year-old girl suspended from school after having had sexual intercourse with several boys was placed under psychiatric care of the defendant. At first, conferences consisted only of conversations conducted across the desk. One afternoon, in leaving, however, the girl was crying and the defendant put his arm around her and kissed her forehead. After this, conferences across the desk occupied only the first part of the session, and thereafter, with the blinds closed, they would kiss and fondle one another. Eventually they had sexual intercourse. She later told a girlfriend and the authorities were eventually informed. Defendant was convicted of statutory rape.

While the gesture of comfort of an arm around the shoulder and a kiss on the forehead may be as innocent as the wind, it is suggested that the spectre of what can happen afterwards and did happen in *Bernstein* would caution some to read *Hammer v. Rosen* and *Landau v. Werner* to condemn this act alone as malpractice. They should be otherwise interpreted.

Rather than formulations of limitation from the criminal order, what binds the rule in *Landau* to that in *Hammer* may be the sense of the psychiatrist's having traded upon his professional relationship to an end not only external to that of the therapy, but directly injurious to it. *Landau,* at least, takes these two steps, and while *Hammer* does not, at least explicitly, Dr. Rosen himself may have taken this issue from the case by his own statement that treatment involving such beating was "fantastic" to suggest. The

57 19 Pa. D. & C. 2d 635, 35 North Co. R. 206 (C.P. Northampton County Ct. 1959).

58 People v. Bernstein, 340 P.2d 299 (D. Ct. App. Cal. 1959).

59 *Ibid.*

test of legally protected psychiatric practice is, to some extent at least, understandable as a statement of what therapeutic behavior is or rather whether a particular course of behavior is medically accepted as a therapeutic medium. The act is the same, in general. Even the *Hammer* court, by its emphasis upon the defendant, Dr. Rosen's, acknowledgment that any mode of treatment involving assaults upon a patient was "fantastic," left open the suggestion that the issue of therapeutic justification was not alien to the decision: that behavior is acceptable or not if it is medically accepted as serving a therapeutic end. Rather than denying the rule, *Hammer* may affirm it by paying deference to it as it indicates its boundaries.[60]

One of the things that these two cases suggest is a marking out of the limits of therapeutic activity as of therapeutic innovation. Their mistake may be in giving too little recognition to the difficulty of evaluating therapeutic strategy in objective terms. They may curb a tendency to see therapeutic necessity determining moral and clinical as well as legal issues. Certainly there are limits to psychiatric behavior. But they are not always so easy to perceive. In curbing the psychiatrist, it is important to see him in his medical role and not as a surrogate lawgiver. He may be engaging in criminal conspiracy when he joins his patient in planning an adulterous conquest, but he is surely not required at the cost of his immunity from malpractice litigation to prohibit such behavior in his patient. This is not because of some special standing he has before the Criminal Law but rather because adultery itself is probably an aspect of a sexual law in the process of transition.[61] It must be regarded as settled that the Criminal Law sets one boundary to therapeutic activity. *Rosenfeld v. Coleman* is but the reflection of the Criminal Law in the law of Tort. The Criminal Law then marks one of the pillars of Tort Law itself.

Medical practice marks another. It has not yet, apparently, been demonstrated that the standard of medical practice is not a

60 Although it has recently been argued that emphasis upon trust is the medical profession's doing and that the Law sees the physician-patient relationship in contractual terms, the traditional legal formulation of the relationship and the tone of decision is the fiduciary nature of the dealings between doctor and patient.
61 *See* Sachnoff: Book Review, 13 *Arch. Gen. Psychiat.* 478, 479 (1965).

useful, albeit not a wooden guide to the malpractice court. *Hammer v. Rosen* underlines the fact that it is only a guide. There are others as well.

Like the courts, the psychiatrist must depend upon the specific facts of the therapeutic situation. Professional doctrine becomes his principal guide in discovering the patient's interest.[62] The psychiatrist may rest with a therapeutic act which is countenanced by the psychiatric profession. He need not pursue a course about which there is unanimity, so long as the minority viewpoint is legitimately recognized.[63]

Nevertheless, in the psychotherapies, where decisions are numerous, minute and critical,[64] and where "standard procedures" may be significantly, if covertly, avoided, so that the very concept

62 *See* Prosser, *Torts* § 32, at 166-67 (3d ed. 1964).

63 *See* Landau v. Werner (C.A. Nov. 22, 1961) in *The Times* (London), Nov. 23, 1961, p. 5, col. 1. The justice advised that courts should be chary of finding a physician negligent merely because his treatment was unsuccessful or contrary to what even a large majority of medical opinion would recommend. *See* McCoid *op. cit. supra* note 1 at 565. "Even where there is an established mode of treatment, the physician may be permitted to innovate somewhat if he can establish that in his best judgment this was for the benefit of the patient and where the established modes have proved unsuccessful." *Id.* at 583. *See also* Prosser, *op. cit. supra* note 61, 32 at 166; Note, 40 *Calif. L. Rev.* 159 (1959).

The issue of whether the treatment given in the *Hammer* case was justifiable innovation or proscribed experiment was not explicitly placed before the court, possibly to avoid the effect upon the jury of an admission of non-defensive beatings. The tactic of denying that the course of conduct was undertaken as treatment appears to have been adopted without quenching all of the brush fires. Thus, defendant's alleged exclusion of the plaintiff's nurse from his consultation room might be causally linked to the intentional application of the beatings. Furthermore, "Mrs. Hammer also testified to conversations with the defendant wherein he stated that the assaults complained of were part of the treatment." 7 App. Div. 2d at 218, 181 N.Y.S.2d at 807.

64 *See* Fisch, "Resistance to Change in the Psychiatric Community," 13 *Arch. Gen. Psychiat.* 359 (1965).

> Conversations are continually being steered by the therapist not only in obvious ways, such as questions, but often by such subtle clues as variations in attention, manifestations of tension such as changes in breathing, tonal emphases, and even the display of books which indicate the therapist's areas of interest.

Id. at 360. *See also* Burnham *op. cit. supra* note 5 at 352. *Compare* Landau v. Werner (Q.B. March 7, 1961) in *The Times* (London), March 8, 1961, p. 5, col. 3: "His Lordship thought that this lady might have read into small and innocent gestures a meaning which they did not in fact possess as a result, perhaps, of the transference."

of a community of practice is shaken,[65] there must be more specific guidelines for the doctor. For example, the psychiatrist must not orient his therapy towards eliciting behavior which will place the patient in legal jeopardy.[66] This is not simply to say that the psychiatrist himself may not violate the Criminal Law in his practice. It means also that should the patient have drug addiction symptoms,[67] the psychiatrist should not orient his therapy towards maintaining the use of narcotics as a condoned means of defense.[68] Likewise, if the psychiatrist indulges in fornication with his patient, it is not simply that the psychiatrist is not privileged to

[65] *See* Fisch, *supra* note 64.

> That conventional clinicians depart from "proper" technique is most usually revealed in small "trusted" groups and as asides, rarely in an open formal meeting. Even so, such asides still allow for the realization that orthodoxy is not all that popular or slavishly followed and younger therapists in particular may soon realize the illusory nature of "standard practice."

Id. at 361.

[66] *See* Rosenfeld v. Coleman, 19 Pa. D. & C. 2d 635, 35 North. Co. R. 206 (C.P. Northampton County Ct. 1959). In *Rosenfeld,* plaintiff became defendant's patient after suffering migraine headaches, nervousness, and general weakness. When plaintiff complained of severe pains a month later, defendant provided plaintiff with the prescription for Demerol,® a synthetic narcotic drug. Upon plaintiff's return from the pharmacy, defendant instructed him in the use of, and provided him with a syringe for injection of the drug. After some counseling, psychiatric treatment ceased, but the prescriptions for Demerol were continued. Plaintiff was eventually diagnosed by the Pennsylvania Department of Health as an addict. The addiction, it was alleged, began under defendant's care. The court held it error to enter a nonsuit since one purpose of the Anti-Narcotics Act was to limit prescriptions for drug addicts. *Id.* at 643, 646, 35 North. Co. R. at 212, 214-15. While the case is initially concerned with measuring the psychiatrist's liability under the criminal statute, the facts include and suggest limits where, as there, the patient is led to a path of behavior which subjects him to the sanctions of the Criminal Law.

[67] Rosenfeld v. Coleman, *supra* note 66.

[68] *See* Menninger, "A Psychiatric View of the Police," *The Police Chief,* Dec. 1956, p. 41.

> We psychiatrists have not made it sufficiently clear that attempting to understand an individual whom we treat is not necessarily to condone all the behavior of such an individual or even to expect inevitable penalties for such behavior to be waived merely because he is in treatment. Not all my colleagues agree with me about this. But I think we psychiatrists have sometimes put ourselves in a bad light by giving the impression that if a man is taking treatment, he should be permitted continued offensiveness without penalty. I am willing to try to help him with his *temptations;* but not with his *crime.* I am willing to try to help a man who is tempted to commit murder or arson, but I am not willing to treat a man—as an outpatient—who can't resist doing so. I grant that homosexual seductions, etc., are less serious than arson or murder, but the principle is the same.

Id. at 44.

break the Criminal Law, but that whatever his right to take his own fate in his hands, he is not legally protected in encouraging his patient to do so.[69]

Although the rules of medical ethics may offer some threshold direction in the search for the terms of the trust, the motives of the negligent psychiatrist need not constitute a breach of ethics for liability to exist. In *Landau v. Werner,* the court absolved Dr. Werner of any professional misconduct, even though it held him liable for malpractice.[70] The standard of the law of negligence is an objective one.

PROOF OF INJURY: EMOTIONAL DISTRESS AND CONTRIBUTORY NEGLIGENCE

Injury caused by a psychiatrist need not involve the specific damage as when a negligent statement is relied upon. The whole course of psychotherapy depends upon a general and continuous reliance upon the psychotherapist to use words skillfully and carefully. The law should follow psychiatry in this judgment. Although it might be difficult to evolve, *Landau v. Werner* touches this issue only tangentially, for there was a damage not so much to expectation, as to causing confused perception about the nature of the relationship to the psychiatrist. It was an injury to specific expectation.[71] Was he her lover, her friend or only her doctor? If he was her doctor, why did he meet her on what appeared to be dates? If he were not persuading her as a lover, why did she feel "in love" with him?

But whether or not the damage in *Landau* was accomplished

69 Kleptomania may be a more universal example because sexual mores in transition have created a sexual law with mixed adherence. *See* Sachnoff, Book Review, 13 *Arch. Gen. Psychiat.* 478, 479 (1965).

70 Whether the scope of the implied contract or representation to employ the profession's standards of skill and care extends to include its standards of comportment and deportment may be an open question. Nevertheless, *Landau* stands for the proposition that ethical professional conduct is not a defense to an action for malpractice. The necessity of ethical conduct recognizes an interest in privacy—something of decency and modesty—rather than a purely medical interest. However, in psychotherapy where, as the Queen's Bench witness in *Landau* stated, there "could be no separation between social and professional conduct," fixing the limits of proper conduct becomes difficult indeed.

71 This is to be distinguished from the general expectation of non-tortious behavior.

by ambiguity or confusion, the harm was felt emotionally.[72] The case thus held that negligently causing mental distress is actionable in tort. It was, however, an emotionally felt injury while specific suggestions as to action or even, it is argued, specific interpretations relied on because of high dependency even if they were intended to be only suggestions, can be actionable if they are wrong—not what a reasonable physician would deliver—and caused harm. The choice in granting or denying this remedy may depend upon the ability of the patient with a given condition to distinguish suggestions from prescriptions.[73] His contributory negligence or in what some courts still consider a budding discipline, assumption of the risk (the argument being that a psychiatrist cannot be as sure of his interpretations and suggestions as

[72] It is now the rule in New York and New Jersey, among other states, that impact need not be made by a tortfeasor in order for emotional injury caused by him to be actionable. *See* Battalla v. State, 10 N.Y.2d 237 (1961); Falzone v. Busch, 45 N. J. 559, 214 A.2d 12 (1965); Robb v. Pa. R.R., 33 L.W. 2648 (Pa. 1965); Niederman v. Brodsky, 38 L.W. 2405 (Pa. 1970). *See* Ferrara v. Galluchio, 5 N.Y.2d 16, 152 N.E.2d 249 (1958) where mental anguish was suffered as the result of information from a physician. The dissent in *Battalla* saw mental illness as encompassed by the majority's decision, though it is arguable that plaintiffs might be discouraged by the embarrassing nature of mental illness.

[73] This at times (and especially in resolving neurotic dependency) is a departure from the classic duty of obedience of patient to physician as an aspect of his contract with the physician.

It is a well-settled proposition of law that it is the duty of the patient upon placing himself in the hands of a physician to follow strictly all instructions and conform to the necessary prescriptions and treatment if they are such as a physician or surgeon of ordinary skill and care would adopt or sanction. As a disregard of this obligation results to the injury of the patient only, it does not give the physician a cause of action against the patient; yet if the patient endeavors to recover damages for injuries which he claims result from unskilled treatment, the physician and surgeon may, by showing that the patient is guilty of such negligence or disobedience, prevent his recovery. Taylor: *The Law is Its Relation to Physicians,* 78 (1900). In such cases, it is akin to an estoppel. But the patient is not liable to follow a negligently prescribed course of action. The duty of obedience sounding like a relationship between unequals, the contrary of which is an important aspect of psychiatric learning, does not mean that a physician may depart from his duty to oversee the case. *Cf.* Howell v. Biggart, 108 W. Va. 560, 152 S.E. 323 (1930).

The patient's faulty perception has led courts to allow parental consent for treatment of adult children for whom no committee of the person has been appointed. *See,* Anon. v. State, 17 App. Div.2d 495, 236 N.Y.S.2d 88 (1963). This was the case of a patient diagnosed as suffering from dementia praecox, mixed type, featured by catatonic and paranoid schizophrenia.

an orthopedist), will differ depending upon his independence of condition or his condition vis-à-vis the therapist.

The classic situation would be that of taking an overdose of drugs.[74] Knowing that a patient is sufficiently self-destructive to do such a thing is the basis for holding the physician liable therefor.

In terms of reliance, we must distinguish the psychiatrist from the non-therapist friend or acquaintance. The one is verbally administering his care, the other is merely talking. But there are categories of words spoken by psychiatrists even excluding the weight given them by patients, which may be actionable. There may be descriptions of dining places, haberdashers, things to say to employers, husbands, or wives. There may be analytic interpretations, or prescriptions for food, diet, attitudes toward parents, quasicriticisms or statements counseling divorce, sexual intercourse,[75] leaving or taking an apartment or job, as well as expert estimations that a psychotic break may be forthcoming.[76] If one is advised to have intercourse even with a prostitute or to divorce one's wife[77] or leave a parental home and the patient is too insecure or shaky to take the step with ensuant hospitalization and job loss, drug addiction,[78] or even suicide, may not the psy-

74 *See* Johnson v. Primm, 396 P.2d 426 (N. Mex. 1964); *Cf.* Rosenfeld v. Coleman, 19 Pa. D. & C. 2d 635, 35 North. Co. R. 206 (C.P. Northampton County Ct. 1959). (Addiction, M.D. continuing dose even after addiction known.) Compare e.s.t. cases. *Cf.* King v. Solomon, 323 Mass. 326, 81 N.E.2d 838 (1948) (morphine).

75 Masters and Johnson: *The Human Sexual Response* (1970).

76 Creating the anxiety that a person may become "insane" has been compensable harm. *See,* Walker v. Boston & M.R. Co., 71 N.H. 271, 51 A. 918 (1902); Smith v. Boston & M.R. Co., 87 N.H. 246, 177 A. 729 (1935). If the fear is created during treatment, the doctor has an obligation to be sensitive as to how the patient will react to such a prediction or warning. Telling a possible patient the same thing may create different consequences. For one thing, the psychiatrist is charged with not knowing as much how such a dangerous statement can be accepted.

77 *Cf.* Salters v. Grant, *Parade,* May 3, 1970, p. 2, where the defendant patient counterclaimed that the plaintiff's treatments "aggravated the estrangement from his wife" after he had allegedly conducted therapy whose objective was to restore harmony to the marriage.

78 Rosenfeld v. Coleman, 19 Pa. D. & C. 2d 635, 35 North Co. R. 206 (1959). Drug addiction may be compared with psychic dependency. It may not be all medical advice.

chiatrist who should have known of the risk be liable in tort?[79] What is crucial in this determination is to be certain that the psychiatrist is only suggesting, rather than advising or prescribing conduct. Different mental states on the part of patients may blur the intended directionality of the statement. Psychiatrists are expected to be aware of what the patient's reaction will be, i.e. how the statement will be perceived and comprehended.

In *Landau,* there is a conflict of definitions if we assume no professional breach occurred. "Social visits" mean visits in which he is not directing his every move for and by the interest of his patient, even in answering telephones, etc. If it were not so, the case would mean only a particular setting or location, rather than pursuit of non-therapeutic ends. It does not mean a patient may not be visited at home or taken on a trip or vacation with his therapist. The presence of third persons makes the functions of groups in this area perhaps a safer course. It is, however, the very vulnerability of the patient and the need for therapeutic judgment on the psychiatrist's every word and act that makes "socializing" so difficult.

CONSENT

Where the treatment has been successful and there are no apparent injuries, courts are reluctant to find a technical assault and battery, even though the consent might not have been granted in the most careful or complete manner.[80] They have thus allowed patients to consent to insulin coma therapy on behalf of a "mentally ill" 34-year-old child, who had not been declared incom-

[79] One court has gone so far as to trace a murder or homicide as the compensable result of faulty termination of psychiatric treatment. *See* Underwood v. U. S., 356 F.2d 92 (5th Cir. 1966). *But, see,* Kendrick v. U.S., 82 F. Supp. 430 (N.D.Ala. 1949); C.J.S., *Phys. and Surg.* § 55 (Supp. 1972). It counsels psychiatrists to be exceedingly careful about discharging the volatile and dangerous from psychiatric hospitals. The case also raises the issue of liability in negligence for intervening criminal acts which by their nature could have been foreseen.

[80] *See* Anon. v. State, 17 App. Div. 2d 495, (3rd Dept. 1963). Indeed in Kentucky, consent to electroshock therapy is not considered necessary, since the treatment is an accepted therapy beyond the stage of experimentation. Lindman and McIntyre: *The Mentally Disabled and the Law* 149 (1961). See, Note, 97 *U. of Pa. L. Rev.* 436 (1949).

petent[81] over the objection that it should have been obtained from a court-appointed guardian or from both parents and have permitted spouses to consent for incompetent mentally ill adult patients.[82] Indeed it is stated that the patient's consent is invalid: "[A] person who is *non compos mentis* is incapable of giving a valid consent, and unless an emergency exists, the consent of one standing in the position of a guardian must be secured.[83] Deciding whether an emergency exists depends upon "such circumstances as the seriousness of the need, the urgency of the situation, and the time or interval of the patients' incapacity.[84] In an English case, the jury was charged as follows:[85]

> Members of the jury, though it is a matter entirely for you, you may well think that when a doctor is dealing with a mentally sick man and has a strong belief that his only hope of cure is submission to electro-convulsive therapy, the doctor cannot be criticized if he does not stress the dangers which he believes to be minimal, which are involved in that treatment.

If this be so, not only is the physician's responsibility of non-influence the greater but no obedience can be relied on by the physician to qualify his watchfulness. This is an aspect of the fiduciary duty of loyalty.

81 *Ibid.*

82 Farber v. Olkon, 40 Cal. 2d 503, 254 P.2d 520 (1953) (shock therapy); Lester v. Aetna Casualty and Surety Co., 240 F.2d 676 (5th Cir. 1957) (shock therapy). *See* Kelly: "The Physician, the Patient, and the Consent", 8 *Kan. L. Rev.* 405 (1960). Courts have acted over religious objections to life-saving procedures to allow treatments. *See also* Levitsky v. Levitsky, 231 Md. 388, 190 A.2d 621 (1963) (court order for consent where one parent refused it and other parent unavailable).

83 Kelly, *supra* note 82, at 425. These persons include a spouse and/or other members of the family.

84 *Ibid.* Where the treatment, as with shock therapy, is intended to release the incapacity, the interval cannot be said to exist. Description of the procedures to be consented to probably constitutes an exception to the rule of privileged communication. *See* Hayt, Groeschel & McMullan, *Law of Hospital and Nurse* 176 (1958) for what is an emergency.

85 Bolam v. Friern Hospital Comm. [1957] 2 All Eng. Rep. 118, 124 (Q.B.).

Chapter VI

The Duty To Act Skillfully And Carefully: "Beyond The Couch"

A distinction may be made between the different types of activities in which patients with different degrees of illness may participate with their physicians. Much depends not solely upon the characterization of the activity by the testimony at trial but also upon the scope of the interaction and the role of the physician during it. In this respect, while physicians have often joined patients for social activities, the total nature of psychiatric treatment[1] suggests that virtually any activity involving doctor and patient outside the office may be subject to professional obligation. Thus friendship between physician and patient must be understood as governed by, and subject to, the pursuit of alleviation of symptom and pursuit of mental health.[2] *Landau v. Werner* must, in the light of diminished proscription of social visiting between physician and patient, be read as outlawing conduct which confuses the patient as to the physician's motive and thus undermines the therapeutically necessary feeling of trust in the physician. It was the ambiguity that Dr. Werner thrust into the curative relationship and the feeling of distrust and rejection that he projected upon Miss Landau when he attempted to withdraw from the social visits that harmed Miss Landau. As long as the patient is under his care, and even after it, the psychiatrist must, because all of the interaction between a psychiatrist and his patient is charged with medical exchange of thought, word and emotion, be subject to his total duty of care and watchfulness.

1 *See* Landau v. Werner (Q.B. March 7, 1961) in *The Times* (London) March 8, 1961, p. 5, col. 3, *aff'd* (C.A. Nov. 22, 1961) in *The Times* (London) Nov. 23, 1961, p. 5, col. 1.
2 *Ibid.*

He need not guard his every action with a non-patient or with all types of patients as he must with a patient receiving psychotherapy or psychoanalysis. The existence of the relationship and especially his representations express and implied as he enters it, create the duty of total care whose scope is defined by the type of treatment rendered. When he is treating by psychotherapy or psychoanalysis, he may have to speak more circumspectly than when he is administering electroshock therapy. When he treats a schizophrenic, he may be forced to act more carefully than when he treats a neurotic because of the difference in the seriousness of the illness and the capacity for self-determination of the patient.[3] But in any event, the obligation of the psychiatrist, as of all physicians, attaches to actions "while engaged in the discharge of the duties of his profession."[4] The obligation is thus stated in terms of what he should do rather than what he may do, but innovation nevertheless is in terms of what he thinks, responsibly, that the patient's care requires or the manner in which amelioration of his condition may best be pursued.

While we are perhaps unable to say that at some point, the psychiatrist's duty to his patient would require him to pursue his patient beyond the confines of the interview room, were the patient absenting himself from treatment because of a broken leg which confined him to his home bed, were he too depressed to come to the physician's office, or perhaps where a patient runs from the treatment room in a psychotic or suicidal state, a physician might have even a public duty to pursue him. Perhaps, also, he might have a duty to telephone or in the absence thereof, to write or visit a patient in order to bring him back into treatment. It may be difficult to formulate a rule for such decisions and most crucially, would the therapy be served thereby, the psychiatrist might be justified, indeed in some instances duty-bound, to initiate therapeutic sessions at another place. Or, conversely, were the theater of therapy initially the patient's home, should the psychiatrist end the therapy when the patient expressed a

3 Thus the *Landau* court spoke of engaging in social visits with a woman in a particular state of duress. It may thus be inferred that a less confused patient might not be able to secure damages for such acts.

4 Carpenter v. Blake, 75 N.Y. 12, 20 (1878).

desire no longer to see him, refused continued payment for the therapy, but admitted the psychiatrist to her home and endured the visits? We would not deny the patient confined to his own room by paralysis a chance for psychiatric aid. The answer is that the law should not here require the psychiatrist to cease the visits so long as the patient's medical interest would counsel continuance of the treatment. In determining whether this is the case, the court should be guided by standards of professional practice. The issue of whether the psychiatrist should initiate the visits is a question of medical practice. It may or may not be in the patient's medical interest at a given time, and with a given patient, to act as did Dr. Werner. But there can be no hard-and-fast rule. At some point, the Law must stop a psychiatrist who abuses the unwilling patient. This, however, is a question of fact. Seeking by a rule, as in *Landau v. Werner,* to forestall the abuses proved in, let us say, *People v. Bernstein,*[5] may frighten the well-motivated psychiatrist from a therapeutically and legally indicated step.

There is some suggestion that what bothered the *Landau* court was the abuse of a relationship formulated upon trust to a personal advantage. It is in such a light that courts will examine the psychiatrist-patient relationship.[6] It is suggested that when the initiative for treatment switches from patient to psychiatrist, a court is alerted to a shift in the delicate balance of interest trustee—beneficiary. What the court in *Landau v. Werner* may be telling us is that the intimacies of the psychiatrist-patient relationship may be all right so long as the patient remains the initiator. Once the doctor begins to initiate contacts, we must be wary of his pursuing his personal advantage, though he is merely acting out the countertransference. Shock to our conscience and sense

5 340 P.2d 299 (Cal. 1959).

6 This was the substance of *Zipkin v. Freeman,* 436 S.W.2d 753 (Mo. 1968), a case holding that various non-office interactions and substantial financial subsistence patient to psychiatrist was a mishandling of the transference and thus a part of the practice of his profession and the rendering of professional services. The case (a garnishment proceeding involving the question of the insurance company's obligation to defend) involved the patient's moving into an apartment over the psychiatrist's office, social gatherings, taverns, skating parties attended together and helping him purchase a farm.

of propriety in the sexual advance of the doctor lives on in the face of our knowledge of the patient's overt wish to be seduced because we see a privilege, largely personal, won by the bait of trust. The concept of undue influence guards the door of the patient's chambers.

In this regard, a psychiatrist who takes a female patient out of his group therapy room and into his private study to tell her that when she acts as she did that day he turns on to her, and thus drives her from therapy may be taking a wrong risk, but not be guilty of malpractice because he was pursuing the valid object of having her self esteem rise, taking her to another room only to guard the meaning of his words. If she cannot then find another therapist with whom an equal transference success can be achieved, he may still be avoiding a malpractice situation.

There is another issue quite apart from that of trust. And that is that the hostilities of patient and psychiatrist may be aroused in the course of treatment in the service of the therapeutic end. The psychiatrist may treat the severely depressed patient by undertaking hostile acts toward him in an effort to create a source of anger and hostility external to the patient so that the patient may perceive the source and redirect his own feelings of anger from himself to the external environment. It is suggested that this worthwhile therapeutic end was at work in *Hammer v. Rosen.*

There has been, of late, an increased importance to the rule in *Landau v. Werner.* Under names of various sorts, groups of patients and their "therapist" have begun to expand the concept of therapy to include sessions where play acting (psychodrama) and exercise of various sorts have supplanted or been included with traditional therapy. These means are designed to break through barriers of fear and patterns of introversion and hesitancy and further to train patients to act with their true feelings and to fully experience life and its sensations.[7] The idea is to show the patient that once he breaks through defensive patterns of

[7] The pursuit has variously been termed "joy," *see Schutz, Joy* (1967) as opposed to the more classically stated "ability to love others," Thompson (ed.): *An Outline of Psychoanalysis* 421 (1955) or changes of attitude, resolution of conflicts and vicious circles; relief of bodily distress, increase in self-confidence and well-being. Maslow and Mittelmann: "Psychoanalytic Therapy," reprinted in Thompson, *supra* p. 565, 590, 591.

non-involvement, of lack of expansion and self-awareness, he may adopt the more healthy patterns suggested to him by the therapy. But the extended touching that may take place involves privileged touching between patient and physician or between patient and patient, which once the patient has consented to is non-actionable *per se*.

The more difficult question is the eating, trip-taking and other encounters together that may make the physician seem liable under the *Landau* case. Fortunately enough, there is a clear literature of permission for such activity, and other than single encounters between psychiatrist and patient, liability might seem the more likely if group patient harms group patient under the apparent subsidy of the physician. The defense here may in part be assumption of the risk for physical happenings or for psychiatric directional harm, the traditional defenses outlined above. Where a psychiatrist should have known that one patient might physically harm another patient in such exercises, as by pummeling, the psychiatrist on the theory of third-party assault cases might be liable in tort.[8] The extent of assumption of the risk would probably not go that far.

Another direction of therapy has been beyond mere sensory awareness and toward more open, gratifying sexual relations. Some therapists have even gone so far as to have sexual relations with their patients.[9] Where the prosecutrix was a 16-year-old girl, defendant psychiatrist was convicted of statutory rape for doing so. No allegation that the action was intended to be therapeutic was made.[10] The psychiatrist having sexual relations with a pa-

8 This has been recognized in a hospital setting. *See* Dugan v. United States, 147 F. Supp. 674 (D.D.C. 1956) (one patient striking another patient). Thus in the analagous case of a patient's striking a nurse, assumption of the risk was apparently not relied upon and the court refused to hold a doctor liable for failure to warn the nurse of the psychotic and dangerous condition of the patient where the doctor did not know of the patient's aggressive tendencies. Bullock v. Parkchester General Hosp., 3 App. Div. 2d 254, 160 N.Y.S.2d 117 (1957).

9 *Cf.* Doe v. Roe, 165 N.Y. Law Journal No. 93, p. 19 (May 14, 1971), where a "former therapist" sought to enjoin the adoption of a patient's natural child. It is not clear whether the relations leading to the birth of the child took place during or after therapy.

10 *See* People v. Bernstein, 340 P.2d 299 (Cal. 1959). There was also an action for contributing to the delinquency of a minor.

tient also runs the severe risk of being censured for professional misconduct,[11] such as being struck from the medical register. That is precisely what happened in an English case when a doctor was proven to have committed adultery with a married woman patient whom he was treating for a nervous complaint. The woman said in evidence that the doctor had kissed and cuddled her. It was stated as highly probable, however, that she had given evidence under a delusion as to what had happened.[12] If injury is proven, the act is evidence of negligence.

Some courts have derived the professional infraction from a criminal act. Thus is *Bernstein v. Board of Medical Examiners,* a psychiatrist's conviction of statutory rape in this case justified revocation of his license for conviction of a misdemeanor involving moral turpitude.[13] The derivation, surprisingly enough was not *a fortiori* for the court.

Recent publication of the use by at least one psychiatrist of sexual intercourse as an instrument of therapy may cause some ripples in the traditional statement of the law. There is also some latitude given in orienting a therapy towards fornication or adultery on the outside by a patient. Traditionally, such criminal activity should not be condoned by the therapist.

[11] This was found not to exist in *Landau v. Werner.*

[12] Note, 1 *Medicine, Science and The Law,* 324 (1964). *See The Times* (London) Nov. 25, 1960. *Compare* Landau v. Werner.

[13] 22 Cal. Rptr. 419 (D. Ct. App. 1962); *See* Shepard: *The Love Treatment* (1971).

Chapter VII

The Duty To Act Skillfully And Carefully: "Taking The Pill"

Rosenfeld v. Coleman[1] presents the situation of maintaining a dangerous aspect of treatment in order to reach a curative result. Like the social visits in *Landau v. Werner,* the case presents an attempt to cure dependency, here on narcotics. Differing with a stated segment of the psychiatric community the psychiatrist treated a manic patient for Demerol addiction which the patient appeared to have contracted during the doctor's treatment. Defending an action for negligently causing the patient to become an addict, the psychiatrist asserted that he became interested in the addiction which he believed was the result of mental illness. He prescribed it in non-dangerous doses to "help the psychotherapy," a widely known use of chemotherapy. Through the psychotherapy, he tried to make the patient understand why he had become a habitual user, believing that if he were successful in curing the character disorder, the addiction would terminate.

The case raises the question of controlled permission to use addictive narcotics during psychotherapy designed to cure the addiction. Without explaining the risks to the patient, the strategy might be questionable. But there is a group in the profession which supports this type of treatment. It is analagous to treatment of active homosexuals. It may be contrasted to psychiatrists who require alcoholic or narcotic abstinance as a condition of acceptance for psychotherapy. What is dangerous here is the risk of addiction as well as the breach of Criminal Law. The case also presents the issue of assumption of the risk if the treatment strategy is explained beforehand. In a situation like *Rosenfeld v. Cole-*

1 19 Pa. D. & C. 2d 635, 35 North Co. R. 206 (C.P. Northhampton Co., 1959).

man, the solution might thus have begun at the outset. The parallel to one theory of *Hammer v. Rosen* is noteworthy.

In general, use of drugs by patients is like any other aspect of prescription by the psychiatrist, though there are special dangers with certain drugs. The psychiatrist must use care in their prescription and abide by the cautionary instructions of the manufacturer. Failure to do so has been held negligence.[2] He must render adequate advice on how to use prescribed drugs[3] and warn of their hazardous consequences[4] or be liable to the patient or third parties for consequent injury.[5]

2 *See,* Anon., "Physician Found Negligent For Ignoring Drug Insert," VI *Psychiat. News,* p. 1 (Nov. 17, 1971) (ignoring indication on ampule to use Sparine intramuscularly to avoid hazardous effects.

3 Whitfield v. Daniel Construction Co., 226 S.C. 37, 83 S.E.2d 460 (1954) (Nembutal caused patient to drive off road).

4 Kaiser v. Suburban Transportation System, 398 P.2d 14 (Wash. 1965).

5 *Ibid.* (bus driver not warned of soporiphic side effects of Pyrabenzamine).

Chapter VIII

Hospitalization

As we have seen, the first act which any psychiatrist is called upon to undertake is the diagnosis of his patient's mental condition.[1] This may be done in a public capacity as an officer of the court or the community, or in a private capacity either as a precursor to treatment or in a consulting capacity. Here it has often been maintained that the publicly diagnosing psychiatrist as an officer of the court or a quasijudicial officer, is not liable to the diagnosed patient for malpractice. Typically, these cases support themselves by envisioning the threat to the availability of certifying psychiatrists of their potential liability for misdiagnosis. Without a great deal of clinical support that this argument is tenable, these cases have probably disuaded numerous potential litigants. But it is a part of the necessary feeling of patients that any doctor being part of a public proceeding is directed by the fiduciary canons of medical practice. It might even be conceivable that the non-existence of a remedy for a physician's tortious misdiagnosis is a violation of the due process clause or the equal protection clause of State and Federal constitutions. Without clinical testing of the actual disuasion of physicians from acting in a public capacity by potential legal liability, it is difficult to make a judgment in this area. In other areas, there is a purported disuasion by the ensuant cost of malpractice insurance. This latter fear has been questioned of late.[2]

Other cases have not been bound by this fear. Despite the fact that breach of contract was not available to them, they have found malpractice liability or liability in tort for misdiagnosis

1 There is also a duty to be aware of the patient's medical condition so that it is clear that psychiatric treatment is applicable. *See* Davidson: *Forensic Psychiatry* 297 (2d ed. 1965).

2 *See* VII *Psychiat. News,* No. 4 (1972).

intentionally or negligently accomplished. Conceptually, some suits have been successful by alleging malicious prosecution. Malicious prosecution, however, requires proof of malice and has no application to the negligent act. Since true malice by an examining physician is probably a rare phenomenon, this means of redressing injury is, in these circumstances, somewhat tentative.

It can happen where the question of hospitalization or non-confinement is considered specifically as the sole question for determination. This may obtain where a public inquiry into the need for hospitalizing a particular patient raises the question. When presented with such alternatives, psychiatrists may overlook the existence of alternatives. They may also misgauge the seriousness of the patient's illness, his capacity to harm himself or others if not hospitalized or the detriment to functioning, job and family responsibilities which such hospitalization would cause. He may be unaware of the "secondary gain" which a patient might achieve —to the detriment of his general behavior—by being hospitalized in pleasant surroundings. Thus time, place and duration of hospitalization may breed different reactions, even though the need for hospitalization may be undeniable. An unemployed patient who is moving in the direction of increased dependency may see his motivation to work stymied by being placed in the relatively pleasant environment of a private hospital rather than being lodged in a public facility. A psychiatrist who is unaware of this issue might be charged with negligence or malpractice if the patient's subsequent decline is the result of the gratifying placement.

What then are the various remedies applied to hospitalization? In the first place is the age-old remedy of malicious prosecution. More accurately described as applying to the diagnostic process, this remedy requires malice, cause and confinement. In the annals of psychiatric law, there have been physicians who, like non-physicians, have been convinced by self-serving thought processes to have their relatives and friends committed to psychiatric care in a hospital. The relative ease of moribund commitment processes made the act of confinement, even against habeus corpus procedures, relatively invisible. Thus moments of greed, anger, jealousy and selfishness have sent people to compliant physicians to have wives, husbands, and other relatives and friends placed beyond the perimeter of fortunes, gifts and influence.[3] Where such physicians have been influenced by such persons to agree to a particular diagnosis or to make no true examination whatsoever, courts have been ready to charge them with malicious prosecution.

Difficulty in finding evidence of malice, the shortness of the statute of limitations, and the difficulty which a patient might have in being cognizant of his plight—his being of diminished awareness, for example, and of proving his health at a past time when all those close to him conspired to send him off to the hospital—have all made this legal conceptualization of limited value. It also focuses more upon the diagnostic act than upon the results of his injury.

Libel, as an accusation of mental illness by single act or by the fact of the commitment process, has become, in a world increasingly used to, if not tolerant of, mental illness, a disfavored remedy. An unusual recent case, *Gasperini v. Manginelli,*[4] has, however, explored the act of libel caused by referring to the father of a patient whose name had no "junior" after it, rather than to his son.

In libel, it is generally held that absent bad faith or improper motive (and even if there be such in a military setting), the allegedly libelous words are privileged when the speaker is a witness in a judicial proceeding,[5] or is a military officer acting within the scope of his duties as defined by law.[6] To allege that an affidavit asserting that plaintiff was of unsound mind was falsely and maliciously filed, is actionable in some states under this rule.[7] It is no defense to say that the justice of the peace exercised judicial

3 *See* Szasz: *Law, Liberty and Psychiatry* (1963).

4 196 Misc. 547, 92 N.Y.S.2d 575 (Sup. Ct. 1949).

5 Corcoran v. Jerrel, 185 Iowa 532, 170 N.W. 776 (1919). It presumably applies to relevant and material words spoken (or written). We focus here on the words, while the duty in the above and many other cases is stated in terms of the privilege that attaches to the witness himself.

6 Taylor v. Glofelty, 201 F.2d 51 (6th Cir. 1952). The court held that even though it was alleged that no examination had preceded the officer's diagnosis of paresis, he was not liable even if he acted from ulterior motives.

7 Sutrie v. Kott, 193 S.W. 417 (Tex. Civ. App. 1917).

discretion in issuing a warrant.[8] Elsewhere it is held that statements by physicians that a person is suffering from a mental disease and is a fit subject for admission in a hospital for the mentally disordered, made in due course of a judicial proceeding for her confinement and which were material to the inquiry, are absolutely privileged and cannot be made the basis of an action for libel though they were given with express malice and knowledge of their falsity.[9]

False imprisonment is a more accurate legal weapon. It generally does not require the expert testimony of a malpractice action and needs only the proof of falseness rather than malice for it to be successful. As hospitals grow more free, however, and follow the "open-door" policy, the imprisonment aspect may confine this remedy to cases where prison-like enclosures have received the patient.

Attempts to charge criminal conspiracy, breach of civil rights statutes and due process clauses have occurred but have not received much judicial approval. A plain action styled as wrongful commitment or confinement may be more appropriate. Here no intended act is necessary, and the whole range of negligence and recklessness may be compensated for.

But there are other ways in which a hospitalization may evoke legal remedies. For one thing, the hospitalization as a treatment itself is questioned by the legal remedies just described. In another view, hospitalization may be an act creating a theater of treatment. In other words, whatever particular treatment modality may be administered therein may be charged to the admitting physician. The acts of any of the hospital personnel may be chargeable to the admitting physician himself who has brought about such hospitalization with an intentional or negligent view of what treatment or care could reasonably have been expected there.

This major distinction from private office practice is the intervention of ancillary medical personnel. Sometimes these people

[8] *Ibid.*

[9] Fowle v. Fowle, 255 N.C. 720, 122 S.E.2d 722 (1961). In sustaining the demurrer, the court noted that it was alleged that no examination of the plaintiff prior to her 24-day incarceration in a state hospital had been made.

cause substantial damage. Thus in *Powell v. Risser,*[10] a disturbed patient was choked to death by attendants and nurses eager to restrain the patient. The physician defendant was found responsible for the wrongful death of the patient. Such regulation of the physical brutality sometimes meted out in mental hospitals deserves a remedy, as was here found. Assault and battery provide a ready legal tool for rebuking such treatment.

There may also be times when fellow patients in hospitals cause harm to another patient by physical brutality. Bordering on the potentiality in a group therapy, the doctor must take care lest he abandon his patient to the unwanted brutality of others. Thus he must make himself responsible for correct classification of his patient so that he is placed in the ward or cottage for living and for occupational and other types of therapy where he will find companion patients who will not be destructive to his course of treatment. Thus it might be harmful for a depressed patient to be in a ward with violent patients kept in tow by straps or other physical restraints. Similarly, he must exercise special care to have his patient placed in a therapy group which will be helpful to him. He has less potential for assuring this than with the groups in his own practice which he composes himself. This judgment is especially difficult because so little is known about composition techniques. Indeed there may be a large area for patient autonomy in discussing any therapeutic move with his physician. The difference lies in the fact that the hospitalized patient tends to be more dependent and less capable of making careful or valid decisions about his own welfare. Thus more is left to the doctor, and the consequent level of his care is more demanding. Indeed it is difficult to envision defenses such as contributory negligence or assumption of the risk arising in a hospital setting, even though this tends to graduate down with respect to those patients who are more autonomous.

The point is simply that there are scores of decisions which must be made by anyone in living and maintaining the necessary balance in his own personality. These decisions range from whether to smile or not to the choice of a profession or a mate.

10 375 Pa. 60, 99 A.2d 454 (1953).

As these decisions occur in therapy, they are exposed to psychiatric judgment and new and more effective decision-making processes are suggested and sought after. In this quest, the psychiatrist may often interject his judgments, and decision-making, especially in the transference process, becomes shared or given over to the psychiatrist to accomplish. But this sharing process is not a static entity, and the doctor and his patient may each take more or less a hand in the process as growth or change takes place and needs differ. Thus it may be ego-alien—contrary to one's own style—to let the psychiatrist decide for himself something which months or days before the patient has rushed to assign. Even more to the point is the fact that the psychiatrist rarely—but probably moreso during hospitalization—makes the decision for the patient. Instead he makes only suggestions, despite the dependent patient's view of these suggestions as commands. The psychiatrist must be especially careful about fostering so much dependency in certain kinds of patients that their ultimate separation becomes the more difficult. This is the kind of strategic judgment which, rather than any one particular interpretation, is likely to be viewed as malpractice by a court (upon the assumption that harm is caused thereby).

The psychiatrist must also be very careful about his own responses to patients and must study his own motives and acts with the greatest care. Thus it has been pointed out that his own hostilities may lead him to choose a particular statement or act which may be detrimental to the patient. The very process of hospitalization may, on the unconscious level, be motivated by a desire to be rid of the patient. While no rule of law now holds a physician to a mistakeless practice or requires him to have complete control over his unconscious motives, he is expected to be an expert in reading the unconscious as well as being expert in interpersonal relations.[11] Since his own study or analysis may give him close experience in this area, it is not folly to suggest that courts, when made aware of these unconscious factors, may tend to hold the psychiatrist to a high degree of care in his every act

[11] Erikson: "The Nature of Clinical Evidence," in Erikson: *Insight and Responsibility* (1964).

and to leave behind the less vigorous care standards of earlier days.

The first and perhaps the oldest category of decision[12] is the action seeking to recover for the injury done a patient by placing him in a mental or other hospital dealing with the cure or arrest of mental disease. These cases fall into different categories. One group of cases is called malicious prosecution, the instigation of an incarceration proceeding by a person maliciously and without probable cause. This type of case focuses upon the procedure which brings about the incarceration, not upon the manner of treatment within the enclosing environment. Very often these cases have been brought about by non-physicians who may often be members of the family of the person alleging the injury. An early example of such a case is *Hall v. Semple.*[13] One difficulty has been the immunity from prosecution of those persons who allege immunity for having been participants in a judicial or quasijudicial proceeding. These cases do not explore the quality of treatment but rather focus upon the condition of the patient at the time of adjudication or incarceration, the latter moment being thought of as indicative of the patient's condition at the time of the adjudication. The cases explore that issue upon the legal doctrine of probable cause. The cases spend a good deal of time probing not only the relations between accusing witness and accused—to establish the existence or absence of malice—but also the issue of the existence of mental illness as it is variously defined in the statutes creating the incarcerating procedure. As a result, these cases are filled with accounts of ravings and other symptoms of mental disease. They do not, however, examine the character of medical therapy applied to the patient, the central concern here, but rather explore the diagnostic judgment of the examining physicians. Thus an interested psychiatrist might review these cases to see the courts' attempt to judicially establish the existence of symptoms which would justify a finding of mental illness at a past time.

The measure of responsibility in the cases is not, however, the duty of a doctor towards an established patient, for the defendant has not usually been a doctor of the patient. In other

12 In general, it may not always be of therapeutic benefit.

13 3 F. and F. 337, 176 Eng. Rep. 151 (Q.B. 1862).

words it has been sternly argued in many of the cases that there has been no establishment of the doctor-patient relationship and thus the doctor could not be held liable by his patient for his misdiagnosis. He has usually been accused of acting in a conspiracy to arrive at a legal finding that would justify incarceration. Cases have been found on both sides of the issue of whether or not a so-called doctor-patient relationship has been established. Surely in these instances where it has not been found, the doctrinal footing has been more secure in malicious prosecution than in those related cases where the allegation has been of malpractice or simply of wrongful commitment. *Ayers v. Russell*[14] has been the leading case finding that the relationship of doctor and patient, the necessary condition to a finding of ill application of the skills of the profession exists.

Certainly this difficulty may be questioned, for while the normal private contract does not exist and while there is a policy favoring the entrance of physicians into this role, it being thought that the potential liability for malpractice would discourage physicians from undertaking this public responsibility, nevertheless the patient would seem to have a right, as would any citizen, to be administered to diagnostically with all the care of any encounter between a physician and another in professional intercourse. There may now be some easing up of the stringency of this doctrine.

Another method for reviewing of the incarceration of the mentally ill has been false imprisonment.[15] In false imprisonment, the issue is directly not the probable cause for a finding of mental illness or danger to oneself or others, the typical predicate findings to incarceration, but rather of the justification itself. The issue is not merely probable cause, but the actual finding of illness itself. If focuses thus on the imprisonment, not on the predicate trial or examination. What must have been established is the falsity of the imprisonment with the burden of proof not on the defendant as in malicious prosecution—to justify the "illness" finding

[14] 50 Hun. 282, 3 N.Y. Supp. 338 (3rd Dept. 1888).

[15] It must be noted as an aside that these cases have only to do with those individuals who are incarcerated in public or private sanatoriums and not with the substantial group of patients who are administered to in their homes, in the doctor's offices or in a hospital setting where they do not reside and thus are labelled outpatients.

—but upon plaintiff. As a result, the form of action may be more difficult to employ. Similarly, even if it be established that the imprisonment was ill founded, it may be that immunity for his participation in the finding may shield the doctor for his role as a judicial or quasijudicial officer as a witness in the proceeding. Where this cloak of immunity is thrust about his shoulders, the falsity of the ensuing imprisonment will not be sufficient to find him liable. This may place in the path of the plaintiff a barrier which is unjust and ill-founded.[16]

Another category of complaint in this area is the wrongful commitment case where typical doctrinal bases are put aside and a simple allegation in tort is made.[17] Libel has similarly been applied to attempt to gain recompense for being falsely called or adjudged a lunatic. Even more rarely, and perhaps in one case alone, a breach of plaintiff's civil rights[18] has been alleged in order to recover for the incarceration. Employment of this remedy has not been successful.

Difficulties in seeing the action of the examining physician as medical in nature, founded in a doctor-patient relationship and thus, in the analysis of these courts, the proper subject of liability in tort if wrongly carried off, limit their usefulness to the act of defining legally protected psychiatric practice. Questions of judgment have seldom been examined. Framed as it is, the inquiry is seldom the therapeutic desirability in the individual's case of hospitalization but rather of his potentiality for dangerous behavior. The standard is external to the individual. It does not have improvement of his mental condition as its cornerstone.

There are other things that are different about this decision. It is not normally made in the course of a therapy. Hence its goal may not be some achievement in personal growth, but merely the tranquility of incarceration: removal of the patient from a place where, for example, he may act dangerously. The relationship, whether of doctor and patient or not, has not been begun

16 *See* Szasz: *Law, Liberty and Psychiatry* (1963).

17 It may be helpful to the person contemplating an action at law to allege a group of these causes of action in order to make a finding in his favor the more likely.

18 This allegation has been made in the context of electroshock therapy.

by the patient. The doctor is called in for his decision, positive or negative, on a given act. In the usual therapy, the alternatives may be numerous: the action to be taken may be the subject of invention. There may not have been sufficient time to establish the kind of closeness which is often the basis for informed therapeutic judgment.[19] No consequence is borne in the therapy for the certification of insanity. The action is confinement, a role not necessarily comfortable to the psychiatrist.

Such factors of difference reduce the impact of these cases upon therapeutic activity. Here there is one isolated diagnostic act, calling for psychiatric judgment upon legal issues. The decision is not unlike that called forth from the testimony at the criminal trial. It is similarly unsuited to the therapeutic reaction and its evaluation is similarly in need of distinguishing. It would, therefore, be a mistake for courts to rely heavily upon immunity granted the physician in these cases, when facing an action for psychotherapeutic malpractice.

There may be something beside these factual differences which limit the utility of the false commitment cases. They rely upon a demonstration of a person's being not mentally ill at the time the certificate resulting in commitment was executed, or its prerequisite examination undertaken. They seek to attribute retrospective probative force to a present psychiatric evaluation of their sanity or mental health. Surely this is a delicate task. But they ask the courts to rely upon little more than this contrary medical judgment. Cases of conspirary, malice and admitted failure to conduct an examination aside, they place testimony to their health in evidence and would have the examining and certifying physician come forward with proof of his examination. Sometimes the finding of the physician and the court itself is viewed as substantiation of the dangerous mental condition, or the finding of a jury, proof of lack of insanity. While there probably ought to be a way to find out the malicious, the conspiring, the incompetent, and the negligent examining physician, the way is not to use what is many times little more than proof of present sanity. It would be better

19 *See* Diamond: "The Psychiatrist as a Medical Witness" in *Proceedings AMA-ABA National Medioclegal Symposium* 135 (1965).

to require proof of mental condition nearer to the time of the certificate, at least giving it more weight than that of the present state, excepting perhaps cases where one day separates the certificate from plaintiff's proof. Some showing of the character of the negligence rather than simply a wrong result should also be required. Mere error in judgment is not proof of malpractice.

But the absence of the doctor-patient relationship is a hollow shield. The patient fallen ill and for whom the doctor is called is no less incapable of requesting medical aid or giving consent. The argument that the relationship is founded in a statute is not less misleading. Much that the doctor undertakes is his statutory, his public duty. The Good Samaritan statute offers immunity by specific statutory design, the proof that it would not otherwise exist, as an inducement to attend.

The fact that seems to lie behind the smokescreen of judicial privilege and the absence of the doctor-patient relationship is public prohibition of, and penalty, for threatening or at least deviant behavior. Try as they might, the statutes making commitment a hospitalization procedure still rely upon a standard of "danger to oneself or to others" or "necessary and essential to public safety." The meaning of public action to protect itself against danger, like the power that justifies it, is large. It allows public vaccination and sterilization. It takes from a man his power to refuse medical treatment.

In seeing the power being exercised in the commitment cases as, for example, a power to prevent refusal to accept psychiatric treatment—a power to compel psychiatric treatment—we should not fail to see the kinship to a criminal proceeding. The action is against a public danger, not necessity. The examining and certifying psychiatrist's role in this process may lie behind judicial reluctance to allow recovery for wrongful commitment. Any reluctance to grant rocevery there is very different from the psychiatrist-patient relationship in psychotherapy. It is the police aspect which gives rise to arguments based on civil rights statutes. The deprivation is of liberty. The doctrines of officer of the court, of quasijudicial action, are brought here to protect the psychiatrist in this role. His role has even been given comfort within the confines of *Gregoire v. Biddle's*[20] grant of judicial immunity to the high-ranking officer of the military in making his decisions.

The therapist recommending hospitalization should not be shielded by the immunity doctrine. The result may depend upon the extent to which public and perhaps personal safety is involved. Some attempt to make judgments upon particular reactive patterns is suggested by these cases.

From the wrongful commitment cases comes a reluctance to hold doctors liable for their diagnostic faults and a respect for the difficulties of diagnosis and treatment in the field of mental illness. In those cases where, however, the courts did attempt to set a liability for the act of preincarceration diagnosis, a standard of care, elucidatory for the more immediate present concerns, was set forth.

Where the inhibition in the contrary line of cases had made a standard of care irrelevant, the *Russell* case boldly refused to stop at the cursory door of establishing a physician-patient relationship. In *Russell,* plaintiff brought an action against two physicians[21] and the Recorder of the city of Albany, New York, for "damages alleged to have been sustained by the wrongful confinement of plaintiff as a lunatic," alleging that "the physicians made the certificate[22] without proper and ordinary care and prudence and without the due examination, inquiry and proof into the fact whether plaintiff was sane or insane." Plaintiff appealed from an order sustaining the demurrer of all the defendants to the complaint. The General Term reversed as to the two physicians and overruled their demurrers, in effect holding that a complaint which alleged that a physician who made a certificate[23] without proper and ordinary care and prudence, and without

20 339 U.S. 949 (1949).

21 The case does not specify whether the physicians were psychiatrists.

Many statutes provide for confinement upon the diagnosis of physicians, others require the diagnosis of one or two psychiatrists, while a third category may specify that one psychiatrist accompanied or not by a non-psychiatrist physician will suffice. Some statutes, with concomitant length of time and circumstances both of patient and of confinement and release, require only adult or non-related incarceratory agents.

22 Of insanity, the statutory prerequisite to confinement.

23 Not the examination itself.

due examination, inquiry and proof into the question of sanity, would state a cause of action.

The court did not, it should be observed, go so far as to indicate that present, or by implication past, sanity would on its face establish the lack of prudence in the making of the certificate of insanity. In this case, after the plaintiff had been confined upon the certificate of the two physicians approved by a judge (the Recorder with powers of a Court of Record), he was pronounced sane by a jury on review of his commitment.[24] In laying down a classic statement of the derivation of the duty of skill and care, the General Term reasoned as follows:

> We think the physicians owed the plaintiff the duty of making the examination with ordinary care. The duty must be measured by the trust which the statute reposes in them and by the consequences flowing from its improper performance. They assumed the duty by accepting the trust. They are not judicial officers, but medical experts.[25] They are not clothed with judicial immunity and are chargeable with that negligence which attached to a professional expert who does not use the care and skill which his profession, *per se,* implies that he will bring to his professional work.

While not generally the practice, the *Russell* court thus derived the duty of examining physician in a public hospitalization proceeding from a core of trust reposed in the physician by the state when he in turn assumes the office.[26] This use of the word "trust"

24 Plaintiff coupled his malpractice-style allegation with the claim of a deprivation of due process.

25 This distinction is eased by a commitment statute which specifies commitment by a judge and two medical doctors.

26 Ayers v. Russell, 50 Hun. 282, 3 N.Y. Supp. 338 (3rd Dept. 1888); Kleber v. Stevens, 39 Misc. 2d 712, 241 N.Y.S.2d 497 (Sup. Ct. 1963) *Aff'd* 20 App. Div. 2d 896, 249 N.Y.S.2d 668 (1964).

In *Ayers v. Russell,* plaintiff had been committed under a statutory procedure after a judge had approved the certificate of two physicians that the plaintiff was insane. Upon a statutory review of the earlier commitment by a jury, the plaintiff was pronounced sane and brought this action for damages, alleging, *inter alia* that he was deprived of his liberty without due process or judgment of his peers contrary to Article 1 § 1 of the State Constitution, and that the physicians made the certificate without proper and ordinary care and prudence and without due examination, inquiry and proof into the fact whether plaintiff was sane or insane. It was *held* in overruling a demurrer that the complaint sufficiently alleged negin this circumstance incorporates the wide use of the term to refer not to the classic trust device in equity, but reflects a more general use of the term then invoked to describe the ambit of duty surrounding almost any responsible party in law. It thus loses some of its conceptual power, although the Supreme Court in New York has quite recently based its ruling upon a quoting reference to the case.

Other jurisdictions, however, have hesitated to follow the New York rule. They have, instead, invoked concepts of privilege to protect the psychiatrist in what they judged his judicial or quasi-judicial role. Even in New York, some suggestion of a limitation may be attributed to *Schanbarger v. Kellogg*,[27] though it involved an examination pursuant to a criminal charge. In that case, a psychiatrist who had conducted a court-ordered psychiatric examination was sued for malicious prosecution, abuse and perversion of process and invasion of privacy after a criminal information upon which there had been a conviction for loitering was dismissed. Although there was no suggestion that the examination was negligently performed and though no hospitalization apparently occurred, the court decided that the examination was rendered in a quasijudicial capacity:[28] "His position, the nature of his duty, the degree of his responsibility and the circumstances involved lead to the conclusion that he was acting in a quasi-judicial capacity." The court's action may well have been due to its feeling that the interest of the patient housed in the physician-patient relationship must yield in a criminal charge to that of the public.

Thus the *Russell* court imposes a duty in New York upon a publicly hospitalizing physician though he be but an officer of the court, of making his certification, (apparently including here the examination because it was allegedly insufficiently made) with ordinary care and prudence. As is customary even where a more modern use of the term trust or fiduciary is applied, the duty was

---

ligence, since in such instances doctors were charged with the care and skill of a professional in this act, relating it to, and being dictated by, the trust of the relationship. But the duty was that of ordinary care.

27 35 App. Div.2d 902, 315 N.Y.S.2d 1013 (1971).

28 35 App. Div.2d at —, 315 N.Y.S.2d at 1016.

derived from the concept of trust. The problem left open by this usage is to whom the duty of loyalty is owed. Certainly *Ayers v. Russell* leaves this question open.

We might, in this situation, assume for argument sake that the duty is owed the beneficiary of the duty of care and prudence. But it is more likely that the trustee stands as a neutral witness in the *Russell* view, stripped of the indicium to loyalty that abides in the concepts of gaining consent to make the examination and the obligation to retain as secret his findings upon it—to the extent which these are aspects of the duty of loyalty. But the *Russell* court recognized that there would ordinarily be owing here the obligation to remain silent about the results of his examination which could only be revealed because the communication was deemed privileged. This revelation to a third party, in non-public hospitalization procedures, (excluding that which would be deemed necessary to secure the proper care and treatment for the patient—and probably only upon his consent), is a breach of the duty of loyalty. It would be privileged here—as would perhaps a revelation in a private proceeding to the patient's parent or spouse if the latter made the request to have the patient examined.

The New York General Term nicely dealt with the problem of privilege by making it dependent upon pursuit of the trust—upon being activated by or demonstrating skill and care:

> It is urged that the physicians are privileged by the statute, and their certificates are privileged communications. Doubtless this is true if they discharge their duty with ordinary care; but in the absence of such care their privilege cannot protect them. Their *privilege* is that, so long as they do their duty with the care and skill the statute presumes and requires, they are not responsible to the plaintiff for the consequences; however harsh they may be; for in such a case the law afflicts the plaintiff, but when they do not use such care and skill it is their personal negligence which afflicts him.

In reaching the judgment, the General Term had to put aside the arguments of the dissent that no doctor-patient relationship existed on which to base the malpractice-like remedy and that by its judgment the court would discourage physicians from undertaking the public trust. It urged that the certifying physicians were quasijudicial officers and that even their negligent actions were privileged.[29] These arguments have appealed to courts of other jurisdictions, although New York has seen fit to follow the 1888 decision.[30]

Faced with this dilemma, plaintiffs have attempted to use other modes of pleading. They have, for example, employed a due process argument. Thus the plaintiff in *Russell* himself alleged that by his confinement until discharge he was deprived of his liberty without due process or the judgment of his peers in violation of Article 1 § 1 of the state constitution.[31] The Court dealt with this by anology, that in the absence of malicious prosecution it is never alleged that a felon committed to await the grand jury is so deprived of his liberty without due process of law. "The State cannot," said the court, "take all steps at once."[32]

Similarly, resort to the Federal Civil Rights Statute,[33] was discouraged in *Bartlett v. Weimer*.[34] In that case, the Court of Appeals relied on the judicial officer's immunity doctrine and the fact that the right not to have private individuals swear falsely in a state court is not a right secured by the Federal Constituion. It therefore dismissed a complaint alleging that the manner of conducting the examination and the nature of the purported medical findings amounted to a deprivation of plaintiff's constitutional rights under the Civil Rights Statute.

Bartlett also answered the question of the effect of at least one type of procedural failure on the retention of immunity. It was

29 Ayers v. Russell, 50 Hun. 282, 3 N.Y. Supp. 338 (1888) (dissent).

30 *See* Kleber v. Stevens, 39 Misc. 2d 712, 241 N.Y.S.2d 497 (Sup. Ct. 1963) *aff'd* 20 App. Div. 2d 896, 249 N.Y.S.2d 668 (1964).

31 50 Hun. 287, 3 N.Y. Supp. 339.

32 *ibid.*

33 42 U.S.C.A. § 1983 (1970) (R.S. § 1979) Act. Apr. 20, 1871, ch. 22, § 1, 17 Stat. 13.

> Every person who, under color of any statute, ordinance, regulation, custom, or usage of any State or Territory, subjects, or causes to be subjected, any citizen of the United States or other person within the jurisdiction thereof to the deprivation of any rights, privileges, or immunities secured by the Constitution and laws, shall be liable to the party injured in an action at law, suit in equity, or other proper proceeding for redress.

34 268 F.2d 860 (7th Cir. 1959).

argued that the immunity from suit would not hold, since the committing court failed to comply with notice requirements in the original commitment proceeding. The Court stated that "a medical witness cannot be held to ascertain, at his peril, whether a court has fully complied with procedural requirements."[35]

Other plaintiffs have attempted to utilize the Federal Civil Rights Act as a statutory basis for a complaint alleging improper confinement. In *Beaumont v. Morgan*,[36] plaintiff invoked the Civil Rights Act to assert that she was wrongfully confined to a hospital on the basis of the diagnoses of several physicians. It was held on appeal that the evidence was insufficient to permit a jury to find that defendants were mistaken in their diagnoses.[37]

The Court of Appeals in *Beaumont v. Morgan* introduced the malpractice requirement of proof by expert witnesses into a non-malpractice proceeding in dicta:

> As for plaintiff's own testimony that her behavior was attributable to physical rather than mental causes, we note the total lack of expert corroboration. While this is not a malpractice case, we think the principle . . . is apposite: "In the usual case where matters of professional judgment are involved, a tribunal of fact, whether court or jury, unassisted by expert testimony or evidence from the profession concerned, should not retrospectively substitute its judgment for that of the person whose judgment had been sought and given."
> Were we to hold otherwise, any person could make out a prima facie case of illegal commitment by setting up his own opinion of his mental health against the professional judgments of, as here, a half dozen physicians. . . .[38]

This aspect of proper jurisdiction in exercise of common law or statutory procedure arose in *Bartlett v. Weimer*,[39] where failure

[35] 268 F.2d at 862.

[36] 427 F.2d 667 (1st Cir. 1970).

[37] The court below having ruled that there was an erroneous diagnosis, but it was arrived at with the defendant's action having been in good faith and conformity with statutory procedures. The court below had spoken dicta to the effect that some of the defendants would not be liable, as they did not cause the confinement, and others would have the immunity of judicial proceeding witnesses.

[38] 427 F.2d 667, 672 (1st Cir. 1970). It was not clear whether proof of the standard of the profession was made to govern the issue of whether a mistake is negligent.

[39] 268 F.2d 860 (7th Cir. 1959).

to comply with an Ohio statute's notice provisions stripped the court of jurisdiction and amounted, in part, to "false commitment." Immunity was held to protect the physician, since he had been appointed and acted as an officer of the court to give his opinion on plaintiff's mental health.[40]

Dicta covered the unavailability of a Federal action based on deprivation of Federal constitutional rights in having no false swearing by private individuals in a state court.

Whaley v. Kirby[41] repeated the general rule that "The weight of authority today holds that the establishment of lack of probable or reasonable cause is a necessary element in an action for false arrest or imprisonment."[42] Normally, said the court, conviction or acquittal is immaterial in an action for false imprisonment. In the companion case of *Whaley v. Jansen,*[43] the court stated what is a strong protective rule for psychiatrists acting in statutory commitment situations (one that does not protect those in the normal office practice of psychotherapy or analysis): "If the officers and defendant doctors lawfully and with reasonable cause acted under [§ 5050.3 of the Welfare and Institutions Code] . . . then plaintiff has not stated a cause of action for false arrest and false imprisonment."[44] This statement includes a reasonable examination prior to testifying or certifying to "insanity," "danger to himself or others," or, as drastically stated in *Dabkowski v. Davis,*[45] "necessary and essential to public safety." Such a finding is not necessary to the commencement of private care and treatment nor is the decision to commence such a program actionable *per se.* In other words, if a private physician consented to care for privately a person who is not mentally ill, only libel or malicious prosecution might lie if publication could be shown, with libel being the riper action here, though rare and difficult to prove. It has long been stated that the burden is upon plaintiff

40 *See also* Morris v. Univ. of Texas, 348 S.W.2d 644 (Tex. Civ. App. 1961) where a medical witness was not responsible for the manner of conducting court proceedings *Cf.* Morris v. Johnson 348 S.W.2d 228 (Tex. Civ. App. 1961).

41 25 Cal. Rptr. 50 (4th Dist. C.A. 1962).

42 25 Cal. Rptr. at 53.

43 25 Cal. Rptr. 184 (4th Dist. C.A. 1962).

44 *Ibid.*

45 364 Mich. 429, 111 N.W.2d 68 (1961).

to show that there was no examination or that the certificate was maliciously false or (conceived or made) in bad faith.[46] For such a court, a claim for false imprisonment is not an action for malpractice for not using skill and diligence in making the examination but is for negligently causing plaintiff to be falsely arrested and imprisoned in an "Asylum" or hospital. Nor is it an action for malicious prosecution where malice (and lack of probable cause) must be proven.[47] Failure to examine or making a casual or otherwise insufficient examination is enough for false imprisonment.[48] Demonstration of the good faith of the defendant does not negate the charge, as it does in malicious prosecution[49] but merely goes to mitigate damages.[50] Mere coupling charges of malice with one for false imprisonment does not require proof of malice.[51] In order for there to be good faith, there must be a reasonable ground for believing that the charge made is true, because malice may be inferred from want of probable cause.[52]

Failure to make an examination deprives a proceeding of jurisdiction.[53] If committed because of the report, false imprisonment will lie.[54]

The *Russell* standard is not without its disapprovers and indeed may be a minority result. The suggestion that the standard of care might be more than mere ordinary care had appeared in a Maine opinion written five years before *Russell*. *Pennell v. Cummings*[55] was an action on the case for making a false certificate of insanity through malice or negligence, thus making the falsity of the certificate, rather than the care with which it was rendered, the gravamen of the complaint. In refusing to reverse a verdict

46 Springer v. Steiner, 91 Ore. 100, 178 P. 592 (1919).

47 Hall v. Semple, 3 F&F 337, 176 Eng. Rep. 151 (Q.B. 1862) *cf.* Dougherty v. Snyder, 97 Mo. App. 495, 71 S.W. 463 (1903).

48 Bacon v. Bacon, 76 Miss. 468, 24 So. 968 (1899). This was a case of a casual examination. *See* Beckham v. Cline, 151 Fla. 481, 10 So. 2d 419 (1942).

49 Miroz v. Kippell, 158 Wis. 557, 149 N.W. 375, 377 (1914).

50 *Ibid.*

51 *Ibid.*

52 Miroz v. Kippell, 158 Wis. 557, 149 N.W. 375 (1914).

53 Beckham v. Cline, 151 Fla. 481, 10 So. 2d 419 (1942).

54 *Ibid.*

55 75 Maine 163 (1883).

for defendants, the court stated that aside from proof of an unlawful motive, absence of professional vigilence and ability might suffice for a verdict. The degree of skill and care required was stated as being "high." Said the court:[56]

> Apart from any statutory requirement, the law would undoubtedly hold the defendants in such a case [erroneous certificate in insanity] to the usual professional liability for due care and skill, and when the serious consequences that may flow from reliance upon such a certificate by the municipal officers [are considered], the imprisonment of a sane person in an insane asylum, perhaps for a long time, the standard of care required and of professional learning and ability to deal with such a subject would certainly be an exacting one.

A court thus sitting in malpractice in psychotherapy in 1961 *(Landau v. Werner)* would have a diversified set of roots to examine for specification of a degree of skill and care appropriate for examination of the treating psychiatrist. That the court chose "the very greatest care" does not mean that it preferred *Cummings* to *Russell*.[57] It may mean instead that it was treading very gingerly in an area of first impression and before the prospect of suggesting to the psychiatric profession that the rules of 1888 might govern a 1961 opinion.[58] It was in a reprimanding frame of mind. For once activity is considered skill and care, the area of mere judgmental error is left behind and decisional consequences are invoked. Thus the inevitable language of dismissal, "mere error of judgment"[59] may arise again in the psychiatric context. In *Williams v. LeBar*[60] judgment for defendants by a court sitting without a jury was affirmed where plaintiff had alleged the wrongful signing of a certificate of insanity without defendants' having made a careful examination, the essence of the *Russell* allegation. The judge found that plaintiff was not insane at the time the

[56] *Id.* at 168.

[57] An English court is bound by precedent but only beholden to and not bound by American cases not directly in point. *Cf.* Vinogradoff: *Common Sense in Law* 122 et seq. (1959).

[58] *See supra,* p. 68.

[59] *Cf.* the business judgment rule in corporate fiduciary doctrine.

[60] 141 Pa. 149, 21 A. 525 (1891) (per curiam).

certificate was rendered, thus finding it false, but he refused to infer a presumption of negligence therefrom.[61]

Said the court: "The most the case discloses is an error of judgment, to which the most careful and skillful physician is liable in a mysterious disease like insanity." But instead of the judicial laxity there inferred from the mystery, the addition to explosiveness to the mystery of the forces being governed has, in an era where the tools of the profession are more sharply and widely trimmed, rendered the standard of care all the more exacting, as we shall see.[62]

There is no inherency in the doctrine of skill and care which makes the statement "ordinary" or "the highest" or any intermediate or conglomerate statement of the duty the more accurate. Such words of quantification, helpful as they may seem to the opinion writer, are not essentially as accurate as the statement in terms of what the profession countenances and utilizes. Such is the derivation of the standard which most courts are and should be charged with. Judicial quantification may be more difficult than renderings from a thermometer. Such exhortations remain, however, frequent in the decisions and stand like blinders to the medical profession. No doubt the most recent of these statements struck its mark in the psychiatric profession. They may be chastening if not accurate indicators of how the practitioner's temperature will be read. The true test is rather that degree of skill and care which the average practitioner practicing in the relevant community brings to his art. If words of degree must be utilized to render this standard, then their exhortatory and merely translating function might be understood.[63]

Nevertheless, it is still true to state that words such as "ordinary," "extraordinary," "the highest degree" and like quantified conceptualizations remain frequent in the attempt to attribute to or derive from non-quantified material the show of scientific exactitude. It remains true that the measure of care which the

[61] It might certainly, however, be evidence of negligence.

[62] *See infra and* Landau v. Werner (Q.B. March 7, 1961) in *The Times* (London), March 8, 1961, p. 5, col. 3, *aff'd* (C.A. Nov. 22, 1961) in *The Times* (London), Nov. 23, 1961, p. 5, col. 1.

[63] *See e.g.* Johnston v. Rodis, 251 F.2d 917 (D.C. Cir. 1958).

law exacts in a particular case may depend upon various factors incident to the treatment. Thus the degree has been made the function of mystery and revelation of the illness, the gravity of the consequences of error, the tractability of the forces being controlled: their danger, the skill necessary to control them or the interest at stake. When such a scaling of duty is utilized, it reminds us analogically of the variations in the standard of care imposed upon bailees having different degrees of interest in the bailment.[64] It may only be that the mysterious, the dangerous and the unfamiliar deserve more close attention than the clear, the safe and the familiar, or that we are charged with higher degrees of responsibility as our own interest in something diminishes before that of someone else. This is the fiduciary mode of thought.

VARIATIONS IN THE RULE FOR WRONGFUL COMMITMENT

There are thus at least five possible situations: (a) correct diagnosis, (b) incorrect diagnosis though care applied, (c) incorrect and negligent diagnosis, (d) incorrect and reckless or grossly negligent diagnosis and (e) incorrect diagnosis through malice and/or bad faith. Only the last three cases under *Williams v. LeBar*[65] create liability, but under *Dunbar v. Greenlaw*[66] even incorrect and grossly negligent diagnosis will not strip away the judicial privilege and a certifying physician would not be liable

64 *See e.g.* J. W. Mays, Inc. v. Hertz Corp., 15 App. Div. 2d 105, 107, 221 N.Y.S.2d 766, 768-69 (1961) (dicta) (liability only for gross negligence in gratuitous bailment); Hobbie v. Ryan, 130 Misc. 221, 223 N.Y. Supp. 654 (Sup. Ct. 1927) (liability for even slight negligence if bailment for bailee's benefit); Ciofalo v. Vic Tanney Gyms, Inc., 10 N.Y.2d 294 (1961) (dicta) (ordinary care required where bailment benefits bailor and bailee). *See generally* Sainer: *Substantive Law of New York* 29-34 (17th ed. 1964).

65 141 Pa. 149, 2 A. 525 (1891). *Williams* affirmed judgment in favor of two physicians who had signed a certificate as to plaintiff's insanity allegedly without having made a careful examination. The lower court found that the plaintiff was not insane at the time the certificate was drawn but found no negligence, having refused to presume negligence from a mistake as to the fact of insanity. On appeal, the Supreme Court wrote: "The most the case discloses is an error of judgment, to which the most careful and skillful physician is liable in a mysterious disease like insanity."

66 152 Maine 270, 128 A.2d 28 (1956).

in negligence; and in *Mezullo v. Maletz*[67] malice and bad faith will not defeat the privilege.[68]

The full reach of the Massachusetts rule is set forth in *Mezullo v. Maletz,* where it was held that neither a negligently performed mental examination and execution of a certificate of insanity nor such an execution rendered maliciously and in bad faith where defendant knew or should have known that plaintiff was sane were sufficient to state a cause of action in tort for the resultant commitment to a state institution for the insane. The reason for the first court's dismissal was the privilege and the fact that a judge's intervention destroyed the proximate cause. The court stated that if it were not a quasijudicial position, at least the defendant occupied the position of persons whose testimony is expressly required by statute in and of judicial proceedings. It did enigmatically state that as long as they act in good faith and without malice, they are exempt from liability under the privilege attaching to parties and witnesses in other judicial proceedings. It emphasized that in performing the duty here, the physicians are not engaged in the ordinary practice of their profession.

The ruling on the second count was based upon the statement of an absolute privilege adhering to witnesses in a judicial proceeding:[69]

> It [359] is important that judges charged with the duty of committing insane persons should have the assistance of medical experts in forming their conclusions. The privilege is a compromise between competing rights: the right of a person to be free from false statements touching his mental condition, and

67 331 Mass. 233, 118 N.E.2d 356 (1954).

68 *Contra,* Springer v. Steiner, 90 Ore. 100, 178 P. 592 (1919) (stating the rule protecting the medical witness who has exercised good faith and been motivated by no malice in making and testifying to his examination.) The action was not one for malpractice, wrote the court, where a lack of skill and diligence in the examination is tested, but one for false imprisonment; *Brandt v. Brandt,* 286 Ill. App. 151, 3 N.E.2d 96 (1936) extends the privilege to good faith statements made without ulterior motive. The Illinois rule applies to a court-appointed examiner who is a "quasi judicial officer" and immune from civil action for acts performed by him in connection with the proceeding. Lindner v. Foster, 209 Minn. 43, 295 N.W. 299 (1941).

69 331 Mass. 233, 237, 118 N.E.2d 356, 358. This was held despite an intimation of a contrary position in *Niven v. Boland,* 177 Mass. 11, 58 N.E. 282 (1900).

> the right public and private of a thorough investigation when necessary by some tribunal before which the witnesses may speak without fear. . . . And, as the defendant has argued, the privilege would afford small comfort to the physician if there was a possibility that he would be subjected in every instance to an inquiry as to his motives.

The second count was also defective when regarded as an attempt to state a cause of action for false imprisonment since the plaintiff was confined pursuant to an order of commitment by a judge and there was no averment of defect or irregularity in the order: "One who procures the arrest or confinement of another on lawful process is not liable to an action of false imprisonment, although he caused the process to issue by means of false statements."[70]

The third count in conspiracy was rejected since the conspiracy statute creates no cause of action for civil conspiracy.

In *Morris v. Univ. of Texas,*[71] a shotgun allegation of libel, false imprisonment and deprivation of liberty without due process of law was not proved, as all acts were done pursuant to what the defendants believed their duties were as university officials and the confinement was authorized by law. The court held that plaintiff must prove intentional falsification by a physician in finding him mentally ill.

An action for false imprisonment was joined with one in assault and battery in *Dabkowski v. Davis.*[72] It was held that the medical statements of opinion during pendency of a sanity proceeding (and pursuant or related thereto or pertinent and material thereto) relating to the emergency commitment of plaintiff and submitted to a court having jurisdiction in the premises were absolutely privileged.

The cases relied upon were those holding otherwise defamatory words privileged. It is probably safe to assume that *Dabkowski* would protect medical statements that were made to a court later found not to have jurisdiction so long as the physicians *bona fide* and non-negligently assumed that such jurisdiction existed. The

70 *Ibid.*

71 348 S.W.2d 644 (Tex. Civ. App. 1961).

72 364 Mich. 429, 111 N.W.2d 68 (1961).

interest in the public safety, alleged as the basis for the *Dabkowski* commitment, would probably be a strong factor mitigating such a mistake.

The cases do insist upon attentiveness or diligence in the examination, even when the court does not specifically categorize the action as one in malpractice, stretching the complaint to include this issue perhaps in false imprisonment on the jurisdictional issue of motive.[73]

The DUTY TO ACT SKILLFULLY AND CAREFULLY: HOSPITALIZATION: CHOICE OF A REMEDY

Falsely certifying as to "insanity"[74] and to the need for the care and restraint of an "insane asylum" has been alleged as depending alternatively upon malice or negligence.[75] It has been distinguished from an action for false imprisonment[76] or for conspiracy, although the certificate must be found to be false. Without such falsity, failure to observe the statute's terms[77] has proved an insufficient allegation: "[W]e think there cannot be a civil action for damages against a physician based upon the inefficiency of the methods which he pursued in reaching and certifying a correct conclusion."[78] "[I]t is not a ground of liability against either defendant that he did not do more than he certiifed, that he did not, besides this, pursue all methods required by the statute as the basis for legal action on the part of the municipal officers."[79] Even in the commitment setting, some courts have held doctors are subject to the usual professional obligation to use due care and skill.[80] This has been the marked tendency of courts who

[73] Bacon v. Bacon, 76 Miss. 458, 24 So. 968 (1899).

[74] Which would have been a sufficient allegation.

[75] Pennell v. Cummings, 75 Maine 163 (1883).

[76] *See,* Guzy v. Guzy, 11 App. Div.2d 1047 (1960).

[77] That there be evidence and the certificate of at least two reputable physicians based on "due" inquiry and personal examination.

[78] 75 Maine at 167-168. In England, failure to visit and examine personally was a misdemeanor. *(Ibid.).*

[79] *Id.* at 168.

[80] *Ibid.*

speak of the severity of the consequences and therefore of the standard of care and of professional learning and ability:[81]

> Apart from any statutory requirement, the law would undoubtedly hold the defendants in such a case [an erroneous certificate] to the usual professional liability for due care and skill, and when the serious consequences that may flow from reliance upon such a certificate by the municipal offices, the imprisonment of a sane person in an insane asylum, perhaps for a long time, the standard of care required, and of professional learning and ability to deal with such a subject would certainly be an exacting one.

Certification is also a manner of speaking diagnostically on the basis of an examination and in the context of proposed public hospitalization. There it has been suggested that there is a strong public interest as well as the personal one described. The court that is persuaded by the latter interest is less likely to think in terms of immunity. The setting is, however, to be distinguished from calling for action on the part of the patient rather than on the part of third persons upon the patient. Since the severity of the acts of third persons has been noted, there may be co-equal severity of the preparatory obligations. These cases, however, hold that there is liability for undertaking diagnosis or for recommending hospitalization or treatment negligently. As was stated in *Beckham v. Cline,*[82] if a physician signs a false certificate without exercising ordinary care and prudence in the examination and without due inquiry, liability (apparently for false imprisonment) is established. *Bona fides* is no defense.

There may be practical reasons for not framing a cause of action in terms of malpractice. Malpractice requires proof of a standard of care by expert testimony for the most part, while malicious prosecution does not. The situation is similar with the need to establish a doctor-patient relationship. Against this argument is the obverse requirement of establishing malice in a suit for malicious prosecution, a need that may not fit the facts. Where malice and want of probable cause cannot be proved, it is necessary to evaluate using false imprisonment (or false arrest) instead

81 *Ibid.*

82 151 Fla. 481, 10 So. 2d 419 (1942).

of malicious prosecution,[83] although evidence of sham or *mala fides* has been held necessary for false imprisonment.[84] The remedy of conspiracy has also been used,[85] as has the remedy of libel[86] and assault and battery.[87]

Still probably in the minority, *Ayers v. Russell* nevertheless presents a sensible way of resolving the problem of locating the origin of the certifying psychiatrist's duty to his patient. So also does it point to the origin of the obligation of trust in the psychiarist whose ambulatory patient is below the mark of judgmental and thus consenting capacity. In *Russell,* the state, through the instrument of the statute, reposes a trust in the physician.[88] His command to undertake the examination and certification to insanity of the person, "furiously mad, or so far disordered in his senses as to endanger his own person," proceeds from all the people out of concern for the public safety. The statute is the exercise of this command and the acceptance of the trust and evidently creates a relationship of settlor and trustee. The alleged insane is then the *cestui que trust.* The duty to the patient goes along with acceptance of the trust which the physician accepts in undertaking the public obligation to examine. The trust is vested in him in part, the logic of *Russell* would hold, upon the representation of his profession that he will bring a certain degree of skill and care to his practice.

The court does a good service in seeing the representation of care and skill as proceeding from the profession itself. One difficulty with the reasoning, however, is that the statute speaks not in terms of examining with any particular degree of care, but rather of examining alone. Nevertheless, reasons the court, when

83 Dougherty v. Snyder, 97 Mo. App. 495, 71 S.W. 463 (1903).

84 *Ibid.*

85 Linder v. Foster, 209 Minn. 43, 295 N.W. 299 (1941); *but see* Mezullo v. Maletz, 331 Mass. 233, 118 N.E.2d 356 (1954).

86 Corcoran v. Jerrel, 185 Iowa 532, 170 N.W. 776 (1919). Slander is occasionally alleged. *See,* Bartlett v. Weimer, 268 F.2d 860 (7th Cir. 1959).

87 Commitments have also been tested by seeking a writ of habeus corpus. *See* Darnell v. Cameron, 348 F.2d 64 (D.C. Cir. 1965) (testing the right to treatment in a hospital and revocation of conditional release).

88 Elsewhere, in *Bernstein v. Bd. of Medical Examiners,* 22 Cal. Rptr. 419 (D. Ct. App. 1962), the trust flows from the license to practice.

a trust of sufficient dimension is vested in a physician, perhaps in reliance upon a *per se* representation that a physician will bring care and skill to the performance of his task, and when the consequences of a lack of care are sufficiently drastic, an ensuing duty to exercise the trust with ordinary care arises. This is the common law duty of the trustee. It is as large as the trust and the consequences flowing from improper performance.

The theory is a helpful one. It abandons efforts to define a contractual undertaking, to find third party beneficiaries when, for example, a parent engages a psychiatrist for his child. It makes expression and implication of the duty of care relatively immaterial. And it recognizes that it is his profession and not any particular act of the physician which implies that care and skill will be exercised in the given case. One may query the extent of the state's role in the representation: its licensing raising something of an implication of skill, perhaps of care. But the law traditionally finds care as the adjunct of skill undertaken. Be that as it may, the help of *Ayers v. Russell* is in making the doctor's shingle, his diploma and his license but the indicia of an undertaking, not the undertaking itself, and in seeing the physician responsible for his acts of judgment no matter at whose behest they are undertaken.

Ayers v. Russell clothes the psychiatrist with a universal duty to bring ordinary care to his practice. Its failure to persuade may once again lie in the nature of the difficulty of reconciling an obligation of professional care to an individual being exorcised or ostracized, in a procedure criminal in tone. Perhaps the more emphasis paid the duty, the less criminal the tone.

As irrelevant as these cases may seem to be to the legal action for malpractice in psychiatry,[89] they are the repository of some early and continuing attitudes on the part of courts towards the doctor's role in treating mental illness. Thus the mystery of the

89 They involve for the most part a one-time judgment rather than a continuous series of acts as occurs in a pattern of treatment where acts are often cumulative. The duty of loyalty is also difficult to apply where the physician is paid by, and bound to the State and the public, as if a threat to public danger would place a psychiatrist acting in these two roles in positions of protecting very different interests.

disease, its intractability and the necessity for treating it with the greatest possible care are all marked in the cases. The standard of care is considered either all the more stringent or, where the difficulty of dealing with it is recognized, the degree of care is allowed some freedom.

Ayers v. Russell has a different understanding of the privilege and establishes a whole new insight to these situations, not fearing the consequences of attacking the lunacy proceeding and those in it and of making the physicians stand the test of their professional responsibility to their patients, no matter what the setting. The argument of discouraging physicians to undertake the certifying role[90] and even of discouraging people from becoming physicians is denied its power. Quantity or degree of negligence will defeat the privilege.

THE DUTY OF LOYALTY: HOSPITALIZATION

A special challenge to the duty of loyalty and an exception to the duty of a diagnosing psychiatrist to do so with loyalty to his patient is his duty in the public commitment setting to exercise public loyalty, making his a *society-oriented diagnosis*[91] and replacing the duty of loyalty to the patient. Indeed some courts refuse to allow any action against the negligent diagnosis of a physician pursuant to involuntary commitment because of the lack of the doctor-patient relationship, which is the concept which incorporates the duty of loyalty to the patient.[92] *Ayers v. Russell* is a tacit expression of the need to maintain this duty of loyalty to a person being examined for commitment.

To urge the utility for law of the non-scientific character of psychiatric evidence is not to dispel its potential danger by virtue of the harm which its inaccuracy can visit on its patients. The study of false commitment is, in reality, the examination of erroneous diagnosis and willful misconduct. Undoubtedly the large capacity for the former has created an apt setting, since the many

90 *See* Springer v. Steiner, 91 Ore. 100, 178 P. 592 (1919).

91 *See*, Hollender: "Privileged Communication and Confidentiality," in *A Symposium on the Medico-Legal Aspects of Private Psychiatric Practice* 13, 14 (1965).

92 It is arguable that without owing loyalty, no doctor-patient relationship can be said to exist.

injustices wrought by the bad faith dispositions are encouraged by the low visibility of the examination and commitment procedures and the apparent lack of the same concern being given release as were given entrance decisions.[93] The wrongful commitment cases pose the interests in people being kept free until they have done something wrong (due process: free comportment) against the idea of the public and the patient being free from danger. This interest is not as much a concern in the private treatment cases.

But there is confusion between the danger-protection and treatment functions, which is perhaps inevitable.[94]

Szasz[95] suggests that it would be irrelevant to conduct a psychiatric examination prior to commitment. Is the ritual of examination and its determination thereupon a farce or irrelevant? He has carried the idea of dignity too far and would consider suicide cases ridiculous as forcing the wrong role on the patient. Cooper's suicide is the ultimate absurdity.[96] Szasz deals at the level of trying to do away with the cause of opprobium visited on the patient,[97] but much of this is inevitable and incorrect, and doing away with commitment procedures is a questionable answer.

PUBLIC AND PRIVATE DIAGNOSIS CONTRASTED

How long does it take to render an acceptable diagnosis on the basis of which the different therapeutic choices or incarceration may be made? It should be borne in mind that precommitment public diagnosis is a qualitively different act from private, pretherapeutic examination. The reason is that while treatment is often rendered and is increasingly the purpose of public incarceration, it has usually been to protect the patient or the public from the danger which he, in the state of illness, threatens. This means that it is a closed-end diagnosis in the sense that the only alternatives available are incarceration or release. This is not the case in conventional private diagnosis where hospitalization—pri-

93 The factor of the concern for danger has been reduced.

94 *See* Szasz: *Law, Liberty and Psychiatry* 169 (Collier Books 1968).

95 *Ibid.*

96 See, *id.* p. 154.

97 *Id.* p. 176.

vate at that—is only one of a great number of available treatment modalities. Moreover, in this private diagnosis, more time may be given to the psychiatric interview and indeed many visits may occur before "treatment" is definitely prescribed.

This concept of separating treatment and diagnosis may itself be a misnomer, for the inquiry of a psychiatrist into the cause of illness continues through many states of the treatment and is a definite and continuing aspect of therapy in the psychotherapies or psychoanalysis. When we contrast the brevity of public diagnosis to private diagnosis, where more time may be available and may be expended, we see why too-stringent legal review is not given public diagnosis.

FAILURE TO TREAT

Another advent of the reform in hospital care has been the recognition that confinement in a hospital has not always guaranteed treatment of the patient. Describing this canon as the right to treatment, recent cases have suggested a right on the part of the hospitalized patient to be treated for his illness rather than being left in cold storage, as it were. It is suggested here that not only will a discharge of such a patient often be called for, but also there may be liability in tort—fraud—or for negligence in permitting such a possibly detrimental waste of time during confinement to take place. It is asserted here that the responsibility of the private admitting psychiatrist must be to assure the patient that his treatment is being advanced by his hospital stay. Indeed he may have a more rigorous duty to oversee the patient when the patient is undergoing the extremes of hospitalization. This points up a sharp distinction from the public commitment proceeding, for in that situation there is no overseeing physician but rather psychiatric witnesses to the proceeding alone. It is helpful when public officers are given the responsibility of checking on the progress of public patients in the hospitals to prevent their languishing there without treatment. The fraud remedy has not apparently been applied to this situation, but it might very well be utilized in a drastic case. Short of that, negligence or malpractice might be available.

Chapter IX

The Duty To Act Skillfully And Carefully: Suicide

One aspect of hospital care that is more prevalent than its occurrence during non-hospital-based therapy is suicide. A common item in the evaluation of any severely depressed person is his tendency to take his own life. Thus psychiatrists are generally aware of this risk in many of their patients. Awareness breeds responsibility and the admitting physician may often note suicidal ruminations in his patient which then must be considered in the placement, care and treatment of the patient while he is in the hospital. It may even be negligent for a physician not to notice such a possibility—or negligent for the analyst who does not have the authority to admit a patient to a hospital to call in a physician. Depending upon how serious is the possibility of suicide, the hospital staff must take special precautions through physical or chemical restraints, and locking of doors, windows and stairways to prevent its occurrence. Not to take these and other precautions such as not allowing patients to roam on the grounds of a hospital may cause legal liability. At least that has been the classic view of the situation. A more recent cognizance of the value to adjustment in the outside world of allowing open doors at the hospital tends to decrease the extent of liability for the occurrence of suicide. Picking an open-door facility for suicidal patients may create a conflict between these views as to legal liability. The better cases tend to visualize this judgment in the same terms as any judgment about a patient, and few hard and fast rules can now be discovered. The advent of mood-altering drugs has also begun to unlock the wards of psychiatric hospitals.

Underwood[1] may be compared with the psychiatrists in *Ken-*

1 356 F.2d 92 (5th Cir. 1966).

drick v. United States[2] who had recommended the discharge of a war veteran from further hospitalization for his mental condition at a veteran's hospital but who nevertheless were held not personally liable for the death of a person who was subsequently killed by the veteran. Some of the same policy of freedom of movement that is found in the suicide cases finds expression here in the idea of early discharge. In *Underwood* there was a clear evidential basis for the chargeable act of negligence. In either case, the rule determining liability is the foreseeability of the injury. Thus in *Higgins v. State of New York,*[3] the defendant was held not liable for injuries inflicted by a mental hospital patient while in the park. The evidence showed that the patient had caused trouble on only one occasion during the 12 years he had been confined in the hospital. There was found to have been no professional or diagnostic error and there was no liability, since there was no reasonable foreseeability that the patient would harm anyone. In these cases, while the duty to third persons is through the patient rather than to him, the doctor's obligation of care is related, though it would not, it would seem, be necessary to demonstrate a community standard of care. Also, unless malpractice causes harm to the patient and on to third persons, there would be no allegation of malpractice.

Just as it has been held actionable for a physician to bring a non-physician third party into the presence of a sick person—and thus breach a duty of privacy having both a physical and an informational countenance—because of the misrepresentation and lack of consent, so it has been argued that a hospital is liable for not keeping patients territorially separate from one another where necessary and possible. In *Logan v. St. Luke's Hospital,*[4] the hospital was, however, held not liable for one patient's wandering into another's room. Likely movement, assaultive or suicidal propensities all place interests in self-respect, freedom of movement and action against ideas of safety, control, inhibiting danger. Courts have not always followed a consistent path, although sometimes a clear error with dangerous instrumentalities available will

2 82 F. Supp. 430 (D.C. Ala.).
3 265 N.Y.S.2d 254 (1965).
4 400 P.2d 296 (Wash. 1965).

allow an extensive causative chain to be linked and recovery to occur.[5]

The difficulty of the theoretical issues as well as the practical problems of prevention[6] combine to make courts reluctant to return verdicts against doctors and hospitals in suicide cases. The limited ability to identify the suicidal person and the need to retain the open ward idea indicates a need not to hold defendants too strictly liable.[7] Much circumspection has resulted in applying the foreseeability doctrine,[8] and relying upon the community standard of care. Thus in *Benjamin v. Havens*[9] plaintiff fled from the hospital in which she had been placed. Even defendants' admission that had he known of her suicidal condition he would not have placed her in the hospital—and thus should have inquired about it as a relevant issue to choosing a particular treatment setting—does not preclude his defending that the standard of care in the community was otherwise.[10] The suicide cases do not always follow the rule that independent intervening negligent acts vitiate the causation of the negligence of the primary defendant.[11] They lean on the idea of discernable tendencies[12] and allow liability from the injuries resulting from an attempted

[5] *See* Underwood v. United States, 356 F.2d 92 (5th Cir. 1966).

[6] This has led to much experiment and theories. One source has, for example, suggested a "helping person" constantly in attendance, "rather than the isolation and restrictions previously thought reasons." Margolis *et al.*: "Suicidal Precautions," 13 *Arch. Gen. Psychiat.* 224.

[7] Perr: "Liability of Hospital and Psychiatrist in Suicide," 122 *Am. J. Psychiat.* 631 (1965). Schwartz: "Civil Liability For Causing Suicide: A synthesis of Law and Psychiatry," 24 *Vand. L. Rev.* 217, 250 (1971).

[8] *Ibid.*

[9] 60 Wash. 2d 196, 373 P.2d 109 (1962).

[10] A particular doctor's attitude may differ from and be higher than the community standard of care. A doctor is not held to his own standard of care even though it be higher than that of the community. Similiarly the standard of the medical community has not absolved one falsely representing himself to plaintiff as being a medical doctor. Thomas v. Studio Amusements, Inc., 50 Cal. App. 2d 538, 123 P.2d 552 (1942).

[11] *See* Wagner v. Intl. Railway Co., 232 N.Y. 176, 133 N.E. 437 (1921); Perr, *supra* note 7.

[12] Annot., "Civil Liability for Death by Suicide," 11 A.L.R.2d 751 (1950). *See* Stansfield v. Gardner, 56 Ga. App. 634, 193 S.E. 375 (1937) where such tendencies did not exist.

suicide.[13] A suicide attempt may also be a culminating incident indicating the failure of a pattern of treatment.[14] But it should not be stressed that a suicide attempt is a necessary indication of the failure of treatment. Sometimes, and especially when the product of a psychotic break, it may only be a low swing in a general upward curve of mood during intensive treatment. It thus may be but a sign of warning or a plea for help, although its meaning does not necessarily negate its actionability.[15]

Like a doctor, a hospital is held to the standard of "good hospital practice" and is not an insurer.[16] Thus a patient on a walk, after a three-month hospital stay, who was considered improved but suddenly ran in front of a bus was not the instance of recovery against the hospital.[17] Patient walks and freedoms are generally the product of the most careful thinking and planning and are themselves therapeutic acts toward accomplishment, assertiveness and socialization. The risks of chronicity stand against those of suicide or violence and are to be heavily weighed in the balance. When careful judgment is not applied in giving grounds privileges and the risk of suicide has been carefully noted, liability should attach. But where no suicidal tendencies are either indicated by the type of illness or have been marked in this particular patient, some courts still state it as negligence to permit the patient to leave the hospital unattended:

> Such statements reflect only an ignorance and a narrowmindness that is reflected in the belief that all chronically ill patients should be constantly locked up and guarded, a concept that is in direct conflict with the persistent trends towards the opening up of hospitals here and abroad. One might say that the case represents the medieval view towards the mentally ill.[18]

Many of the cases involve sudden movements to jump into bodies of water, or patients throwing themselves before motor

[13] *Ibid.*

[14] *See* Landau v. Werner.

[15] "Suicide attempts and gestures are often used in a frankly manipulative manner and with some degree of success" quoted Perr, *supra,* note 8 at 634.

[16] Perr, *supra* note 8 at 632.

[17] Mills v. Society of N. Y. Hosp., 270 N.Y. 594, 1 N.E.2d 346 (1936).

[18] Perr, *supra* note 8 at 633.

vehicles or subways[19] or out of buildings. As one author has stated: "The basic law on sudden impulse cases involves questions of foreseeability and controllability."[20] Like the situation with electroshock and insulin-type therapy, the most careful precautions and the highest vigilence do not guarantee freedom from suicide.[21] It often occurs anyway. There is a difference between general predictability in a certain type of patient or illness and identifying the risk in any one particular patient.[22] The predictive judgment may have to be intuitive in nature.[23] The problem of control and, expectedly, the finding of liability is more difficult in office patients' cases.

Generally, the failure to exercise proper precautions when called for is considered a lack of due care[24] and may be demonstrated by placing a known and recorded suicidal risk in a general ward when a special maximum-security building for suicidal patients is available.[25] In such patients both inside[26] and outside of the hospital, it is important not to allow pills to be hoarded and not to leave them alone for too long a period.[27] But hospitals have not been held to impossible duties:

> The State could not have provided an employee to watch every move made by this man during 24 hours of the day. We are not persuaded that it is evidence of negligence that he was not repeatedly wakened and his bed searched during the night. If institutions for the mentally ill are required to take all of the precautions contended for in this case and are to be held liable for such delicate mistakes in judgment, patients would be kept in strait jackets or some other form of strict confinement which would hardly be conducive to recovery. No reason is asserted that decedent was not given suitable electric shock treatment, tranquilizers or other treatment designed to mitigate mental

19 Katz v. State, 46 Misc. 2d 61, 258 N.Y.S.2d 912 (Ct. Claims 1965).

20 Perr, *supra* note 8 at 633.

21 Wall, J. H.: "The Psychiatric Problem of Suicide," 101 *Am. J. Psychiat.*, 404 (1944), quoted Perr, *supra* note 8 at 636.

22 *Ibid.*

23 Perr, *supra* note 8.

24 Collins v. State, 23 App. Div. 2d 898, 258 N.Y.S.2d 938 (3rd Dept. 1965).

25 *Ibid.* The dissent stated the general "open ward" theory.

26 Hirsh v. State, 8 N.Y.2d 125, 168 N.E.2d 372 (1960).

27 *See* Katz v. State, 46 Misc. 2d 61, 258 N.Y.S.2d 912 (Ct. Claims 1965).

> depression and self-destructive tendencies. Reasonable care is required to protect such patients against themselves . . . but no evidence of lack of it has been shown in this case. An ingenious patient harboring a steady purpose to take his own life cannot always be thwarted.[28]

Mere suicidal ideation, having been informed of attempted suicide at home and hoarding of pills with the intent of taking them for suicidal effect is not enough to create liability of the state for subsequent suicide after the patient was placed in a semi-open ward.[29] In *Katz v. State* it was the medical judgment of the staff that the patient was neither a patient with suicidal tendencies nor a suicidal risk.[30] It was conceded that they were qualified doctors and were entitled to their medical opinions.[31]

[28] Hirsh v. State, 8 N.Y.2d 125, 168 N.E.2d 372 (1960). *See* White v. U.S., 244 F. Supp. 127 (D.C. Va. 1965).
[29] Katz v. State, 46 Misc. 2d 61, 258 N.Y.S.2d 912 (Ct. Claims 1965).
[30] 46 Misc. 2d at 62, 63, 258 N.Y.S.2d at 913, 914.
[31] 46 Misc. 2d at 63, 258 N.Y.S.2d at 914.

Chapter X

Administration Of Shock Therapy

Another form of treatment that subjects psychiatrists to malpractice liability is electroshock and insulin-shock therapy. This method of treatment is more recent than simple incarceration. It has often been undertaken in the hospital setting and has involved the legal questioning of incidents to the treatment which are very far from the typically psychiatric. Thus the giving of x-rays after the therapy, the guiding of walking, the use of straps to hold the patient down and the warning to the patient of the high risk of injury have all been causes for reproaching and bringing an action against the treatment group. Nevertheless, these cases have likewise been the theater of attitudes toward the psychiatric patient, not always dissimilar from those found in the commitment cases. What is most striking, however, is the fact that these cases of physical treatment have been the first really modern incidence of actions against psychiatrists for their maltreatment of patients. It may be that actions which deal with the physical are more readily invoked when legal doctrine is attempting to accommodate a new form of human activity. Even so, the reluctance in these cases to employ the doctrine of *res ipsa loquitur* may symbolize a general hesitancy to find the doctor liable for his treatment of mental patients by accepted means.

Quite interesting among the cases is the realization that the gaining of appropriately informed consent from the patient has itself been seen as a cause for action in malpractice. It may be an early non-physical means of accommodating a cause of action in malpractice for a non-physical injury.

From these cases, we may derive a statement of the Law's prerequisite for the finding of malpractice. These are the recent string of cases dealing with psychiatrists and other practitioners in the war against mental illness as they have employed the shock therapies. Shock therapy, referring to drug-induced or electrically imposed states of shock, is a method of breaking through the patient's theretofore methods of defense and thus shaking him free to adopt new and more efficient ones. This is at least one of many statements of their intent and effect. Classically stated, electroshock and insulin shock therapies enjoyed a vogue in the treatment of mental illness in the later years of such treatment and before the psychopharmacological treatment with tranquilizing drugs began to serve as an adjunct to, or a substitute for, psychoanalysis and psychotherapy. One way of stating the function of these shock treatment modes is to indicate that electroshock therapy has been characterized as a method of building up a patient's "defenses and controls and self-confidence" and that insulin shock therapy has been a method of relieving "basic anxiety" and "disturbance of the mood." In either event, the shock phenomenon shakes the personality loose from its former moorings and launches it on a hopefully healthier course. Sometimes they are invoked as aspects of a more verbally oriented treatment. At other times, they constitute the only treatment mode utilized. What is significant about them for legal purposes is that their application involves certain dangers, dangers not only realized in the application and denouement of the therapy itself but dangers in follow-up care as well which exist without regard to the degree of care exercised by the physician or those to whom its administration has been delegated.[1] Indeed so prevalent are such dangers that the introduction to the therapy of the patient itself involves a touchy theater for malpractice.[2] This is because the balancing of the interest of the patient in full disclosure and the interest of the psychiatrist in encouraging the patient to take on the treatment must be carefully done before mutually protective and accurate communication can take place.

[1] *E.g.*, Farber v. Olkon, 40 Cal. 2d 503, 511, 254 P.2d 520, 524-25 (1953); Quinley v. Cocke, 183 Tenn. 428, 439, 192 S.W.2d 992, 997 (1946).

[2] *See* Lester v. Aetna Cas. & Sur. Co., 240 F. 2d 676, 679 (5th Cir. 1957); Woods v. Brumlop, 71 N. Mex. 221, 227, 377 P.2d 520, 524-25 (1962); Shartel & Plant, *The Law of Medical Practice* 12-13 (1959); Kelly, "The Physician, The Patient, & The Consent," 8 Kan. L. Rev. 405, 424-26 (1960) (all requiring explanation and consent).

SHOCK THERAPY: THE TENETS OF LIABILITY

The liability of the psychiatrist, as of any physician against whom an allegation of malpractice has been lodged, is for breach of his duty of rendering to his patient the skill and care, or exercising in behalf of the patient the skill and care, of a qualified psychiatrist practicing in that school of psychiatry in that community; and of having proximately caused injury to his patient by failing to do so. The patient himself must be free of himself having contributed to the damaging act by his own negligence, by having consented to the therapy with the chance of injury, and not having assumed the risk extant in the therapeutic event. These are well settled principles enunciated in the non-psychiatric literature and not really challenged upon such a statement by any version or variety of malpractice claim. The standard of care has been recently generalized in *Johnston v. Rodis*,[3] a case where one of the arms of a patient who had undergone electroshock therapy had been fractured in the process. Not a novel event in such treatment, the injury induced the patient nevertheless to bring a cause of action in malpractice. In holding that *res ipsa loquitur* and breach of warranty, grounds for the later reversal, would not apply, the court stated the governing rule for finding malpractice:[4]

> A physician or surgeon is obliged to exercise the degree of care and skill that is ordinarily employed by members of the profession in the same line of practice in his own or similar localities. Failure to use such care or skill constitutes negligence. On the other hand, he is not an insurer of health or a guarantor of results. He undertakes only to abide by the prevailing standards and to utilize the skill possessed generally by others practicing in his field and to accord the care that they would ordinarily extend in similar circumstances. He must have latitude for the exercise of reasonable judgment, and is not liable for a mere error in his decisions. A patient who claims to have been injured by his negligence, has the burden of proving by a preponder-

3 151 F. Supp. 345 (D. D.C. 1957), *rev'd on other grounds,* 251 F.2d 917 (D.C. Cir. 1958). *See also,* Tobias v. Manhattan Eye and Ear Hospital, 28 App. Div. 2d 972, 283 N.Y.S.2d 398 (1967).

4 *Id.* at 346-347. Care may even mean the manner in which one reaches a judgment. The lack of care need not rise to bad faith, the use of improper motive.

> ance of the evidence that the defendant departed from the applicable standards or was unskillful or negligent.

Even when the intrusion is intentional, the marks of permissible practice are scored with the same touchstone of authority. This is in accord with stated authority.

The electroshock therapy cases present a different preoccupation. Their concern has been with a procedure for the treatment of mental illness which, perhaps unlike the psychotherapies, has a recognized risk of injury built into it. Electroshock therapy produces convulsions in a small percentage of cases. These cause fractures in the bones of the patient, and for such injuries, malpractice actions have been brought against the physician supervising the administration of the therapy. The currency of the treatment, the frequency of injury, and the relative similarity to traditional categories of malpractice gave considerable vogue to the action for psychiatric malpractice based upon fractures resulting from electroshock-induced convulsion. Many of the issues considered on appeal concerned the proof of plaintiff's case by the doctrine of *res ipsa loquitur.* Most courts found the doctrine inapplicable, though its use does have suggestive possibilities for the mental patient whose consciousness is diminished. It would be a mistake to employ the doctrine where lack of improvement, decline into psychosis or even error in psychiatric judgment occur because these are not reliable indications of negligence. Indeed, the danger of such an assumption makes use of *res ipsa loquitur* in most actions for psychotherapeutic malpractice inadvisable. For that proposition, the electroshock therapy cases present strong precedent.

A second concern of these cases was the scope of the patient's consent. Had the physician informed him of the possibility of convulsion and fracture? Was he given the opportunity to discount its likelihood in deciding to undergo the treatments? Would the disclosure of the possibility of fracture itself cause alarm in the patient and so itself increase the risk "by reason of the psychological results of the apprehension itself?" Is failure of disclosure itself malpractice?

Certainly the advance of the cases to the point where informing the patient was not seen simply as a condition of consent to medical treatment but as itself a part of the psychiatrist's therapeutic response to his patient marked not only the evolution of doctrine but a fuller understanding of the psychiatrist's responsibility to his patient. When it was recognized that accurately informing a patient of the risk of a given therapy might in itself constitute malpractice, the complicated delicacy of psychiatric decision had begun to gain recognition in the courts. For the measuring of the potential effect upon the patient of a given course of treatment constitutes the task of both psychiatrist and court.

In its charge to the jury in *Bolam v. Friern Hospital Committee*[5] such recognition is made:

> Members of the jury, though it is a matter entirely for you, you may well think that when a doctor is dealing with a mentally sick man and has a strong belief that his only hope of cure is submission to electro-convulsive therapy, the doctor cannot be criticized if he does not stress the dangers, which he believes to be minimal, which are involved in that treatment.

The view that the duty of a medical practitioner in these circumstances does not necessarily extend to warning of the risks of proposed treatment unless the patient inquires, accords with Canadian authority, said the court. Reading *Woods v. Brumlop*[6] as a gloss upon *Bolam v. Friern Hospital Committee,* we may well question that medical silence must be broken upon inquiry:

> Some courts have held that another exception [to the rule requiring a disclosure of the dangers of a treatment procedure] is where an explanation of every risk attendant upon a treatment procedure may well result in alarming a patient who is already apprehensive and who may, as a result, refuse to undertake surgery or a treatment in which there is minimal risk or where such disclosure may result in actually increasing the risk by reason of the psychological results of apprension itself. Actually some courts recognize a further exception that each patient is to be treated as a separate problem on the theory that the patient's mental and emotional condition is important, and that

5 [1957] 2 All E.R. 118 (Q.B.).

6 71 N.M. 221, 377 P.2d 520 (1962).

> a certain amount of discussion consistent with full disclosure of facts necessary to an informed consent should be employed.

The question, said the court, was "whether a disclosure of the risks involved in the treatment would alarm an emotionally upset and apprehensive patient to the extent that it would not be proper medical practice to disclose such risks to the plaintiff."

What is more striking about these cases which arose most typically upon an allegation that *res ipsa loquitur* should be applied is the coming of the merely verbal instance of malpractice. (This could be found in a non-therapeutic exchange as opposed to the verbal directions which accompany a treatment as, for example, the giving of drugs.) *Woods v. Brumlop* is a case in point. In *Brumlop,* plaintiff had been referred to defendant for psychiatric care. After consultation and some routine psychiatric treatments (apparently psychotherapy), defendant advised that plaintiff should submit to electroshock treatments. Another psychiatrist instituted the treatments and plaintiff claimed that he suffered a compression fracture to the spine and loss of hearing as a result. It was alleged that defendant, who did not administer the treatment, failed to inform and advise plaintinff of the inherent dangers in the treatment, and upon direct inquiry, informed her that harmful results would not occur, knowing that statement to be untrue and that plaintiff had no knowledge of that fact. This resulted in plaintiff having no basis upon which to predicate her consent to the treatments. At one point she characterized her complaint as one in misrepresentation and surely when the purely verbal tort is referred to, fraud lurks in the background. It was *held* that there was no error in denying defendant's motion for a directed verdict. The court stated its result this way: A physician who misleads a patient by not only failing to give a warning of reasonable and recognized risks inherent in a treatment after which the patient would have refused the treatment but by affirmatively assuring her that there are no risks, knowing such statement to be untrue, is liable for the harmful consequences of the treatment. Such a failure to disclose, or the giving of an untrue answer as to the probable consequences of a treatment, constitutes malpractice; and a doctor who fails to so advise his client or gives an untrue answer as to such consequences is liable for malpractice unless his failure to do so comes within one of the exceptions to the rule requiring candor and disclosure.

The courts had been apt to grant recompense for physical invasion. *Powell v. Risser*[7] and *Bellandi v. Park Sanatarium*[8] are virtually companion cases of physical invasion and abuse. But what is patently established in *Brumlop* is a duty of candor and truthfulness. Such are obligations of the fiduciary, and in such a sense may we understand the context and nature of the duty of the physician to his patient.[9]

[7] 375 Pa. 60, 99 A. 2d 454 (1953) (injury to hands from wetpack). *Maben v. Rankin*, 55 Cal. 2d 139, 358 P. 2d 681 (1961), pointed out that force is not actionable in all cases.

[8] 214 Cal. 472, 6 P.2d 508 (1931) (death by choking employed to restrain patient).

[9] Another path to recovery in these circumstances is presented by *Johnston v. Rodis*, 151 F. Supp. 345 (D.D.C. 1957), *rev'd on other grounds*, 251 F.2d 917 (D.C. Cir. 1958), where it was held that the assurance from doctor to patient that "everything would be all right" constituted an actionable warranty. *Woods v. Brumlop* arises in an intentional tort situation rather than one of negligence.

Chapter XI

The Role of The Courts

The price of recognizing a cause of action for psychiatric malpractice is some judicial ordering of psychiatric behavior. At times this can be quite problematic. In the view of the Court of Appeal in *Landau v. Werner,* for example, the course which Dr. Werner should have taken upon discovering that his patient had fallen in love with him was to abandon the therapy. It is settled, however, that the evocation of feelings such as those which Miss Landau experienced is not the signal for termination of the relationship. On the contrary, such intensity of feeling is not only the mark of some therapeutic success but the prelude to insight on the part of the patient. Such a resurrection of the repressed feelings of childhood allows the intellectual and emotional examination of feelings not previously understood or dealt with. Through such reexamination the emotional learning of psychotherapy occurs.[1] Uncertain of the effects of this process,[2] the court could not accept Dr. Werner's judgment that a relapse would probably accompany Miss Landau's removal from his influence. It would not visualize the social visits as his sincere attempt to find a therapeutic solution to the problem of gratifying the patient's dependency need while at the same time fostering independence.

The reason may have something to do with the fact that the medical testimony before the court was taken as a uniform condemnation of social visits. Such uniformity may have been only an accident of proof. That testimony for Dr. Werner's technique

[1] *See* Witenberg, Rioch and Mazer: "The Interpersonal and Cultural Approaches," in 2 *Amer. Handbook Psychiat.* 1417, 1426 (Arieti ed. 1959).

[2] "She was ashamed and baffled at the way her affection had developed towards a married man with two children. It was something that was perhaps inherent in the system of treatment of transference." (C.A. Nov. 22, 1961) in *The Times* (London), Nov. 23, 1961, p. 5, col. 1.

may have been difficult to obtain is not only witness to the reluctance of physicians generally to testify in malpractice cases[3] but is a special problem in the proof of the standard of practice in the relevant psychiatric community.

Although not explicitly in response to these facts, courts have not required expert testimony to establish that behavior "whose very nature bespeaks improper treatment and malpractice" is wrongful. In *Hammer v. Rosen,* the Court of Appeals held that it was error not to submit the issue of malpractice to the jury, even though there had been no expert testimony to the fact. The testimony of three witnesses that the defendant had beaten his patient on a number of occasions made out a prima facie case.[4] This rule has been elsewhere recognized in cases of psychiatric malpractice where severe assaults have resulted in physical injury to the patient.[5] Following it, in cases of emotional injury might create more of a problem. In either case, expert testimony can rebut the prima facie case. To the extent that the court's answer in *Landau v. Werner* reflects uneasiness in handling psychiatric doctrine, repeated dealings with psychiatric malpractice situations may dispel some uncertainty. Routinization of psychiatric procedure may eliminate the rest. Nevertheless, the extent of sometimes covert innovation within the psychiatric community suggests that procedures such as those of Drs. Rosen and Werner may persist.[6]

Gasperini v. Manginelli[7] sets to rest the possibility that the delicacy of psychiatric judgment necessitates the calling in of a consultant. What would have been essentially a hedge, no real

[3] *See* Note, "Malpractice and Medical Testimony, 77 *Harv. L. Rev.* 333 (1963).

[4] *See* page 62 *supra.*

[5] Bellandi v. Park Sanitarium Ass'n, 214 Cal. 472, 6 P.2d 508 (1931) (death by choking employed to restrain patient); Burton v. Leftwich, 123 So. 2d 766 (La. Ct. App. 1960) (assault and battery upon child patient employed to keep her still while removing sutures); a physician need not stand for all abuse, even from a child. Anon., "Boy Golfer, 11, Held as Liable as Adult For Injurying Player," *New York Times,* Nov. 5, 1968, p. 45, col. 7; Note, 77 *Harv. L. Rev.* 333, 346 n.81 (1963). The doctrine of *res ipsa loquitur* is sometimes applied in this context. *See* Sawyer v. Jewish Chronic Disease Hosp., 234 N.Y.S.2d 372, 374 (Sup. Ct. 1962).

[6] *Compare* Fisch, *supra* note 64, p. 83, at 362.

[7] 196 Misc. 547, 92 N.Y.S.2d 575 (Sup. Ct. 1949).

solution to the difficulties of judgment, was foreclosed. In *Gasperini,* plaintiff claimed, *inter alia* that the psychiatrist had broken his duty to his patient since "such treatment as was rendered by defendant was commenced without consulting another psychiatrist. . . ." Said the court: "Defendant was himself a psychiatrist who had been called in by the family physician. It is understandable that he did not see the need for a consulting psychiatrist." This does not mean that there may not be situations in which consultation should be undertaken and perhaps even at the risk of being in malpractice. *Landau v. Werner* may include such circumstances.

Gasperini contains the intriguing aside of reexamination of the psychiatrist's fee, openly facing what *Hammer v. Rosen* and other cases only tangentially suggest. In such instances, the fact that large sums of money have been expended and no demonstrable amelioration of the patient's condition has occurred is at least mentioned by the court, if not taken as a persuading factor in the determination of the litigation. In *Gasperini,* plaintiff alleged that while defendant was treating him, he demanded and received 8,350 dollars "which defendant falsely and fraudulently represented to be a fair fee for which he would render certain services; that he did not render such services." The court denied defendant's motion to strike this allegation as sham, frivolous and legally insufficient, but the court was not persuaded in plaintiff's behalf by the allegation that defendant "threatened to cease attending plaintiff if he were not paid part of his fee." The court stated instead that the psychiatrist "is entitled to be compensated for his work when patient is of sufficient means to pay therefor." The case does not, however, mean that when a consultant or replacing physician is brought in, the original physician should not furnish accurate and adequate information on the state of the patient's health and treatment. Not to do this would create liability in tort.[8]

[8] Underwood v. United States, 356 F.2d 92 (5th Cir. 1966) creating a very extensive potential liability. In *Underwood,* a mentally ill airman who had been hospitalized was released to duty which gave him access to weapons. This negligence, coupled with negligently permitting him to draw a pistol and ammunition with which he shot and killed his former wife, was proximately connected with her death. The

Conclusion

Through unfamiliarity with mental illness and psychiatry and because of problems in the nature and development of psychiatry itself, the few cases in which courts have considered psychiatric malpractice provide only limited and sometimes confusing guidelines to the medical profession. Continued litigation may provide more clarity. Some aspects of malpractice as they have emerged in the decided cases between psychiatrist and patient have been considered. It has been suggested that because the concept of trust plays so large a part in psychotherapy—and as a tool of legal analysis admits the concept of preferential interest—it should be explored as a guide to deciding cases of malpractice concerning the therapeutic relationship. The medical profession itself can provide standards for judging the patient's interest in a given case. Countertransference might then be regulated, and the limits of psychiatric activity delineated by requiring the psychiatrist continually to prefer the interest of his patient to his own. Nevertheless, the extensive liability in *Underwood v. United States* suggests that courts may be quite severe in governing the relationship of psychiatrist and patient, especially where the threat of violence is great.

---

court held that the negligence of an Air Force psychiatrist who first treated him in not informing a second psychiatrist who took over his treatment of the patient's threats on his wife's life was not a "discretionary function" within the exception from the Federal Tort Claims Act based on failure to perform a discretionary function. *See* 28 U.S.C.A. § 2680 (a). Similarly, not to treat at all but only to render custodial care has been held to create liability. Whitree v. State, 56 Misc. 2d 693, 290 N.Y.S.2d 486 (1968). Treating psychiatrists are not, however, required to retain patients under their care under all circumstances. *See e.g.* Fernandez v. Baruch, 52 N.J. 127, 244 A.2d 109 (1968).

INDEX OF CASES

AUTHOR INDEX

the Right to Know," *Proceedings of ABA Section of Insurance, Negligence and Compensation Law* 396 (1967), 44, 46
Shartel & Plant: *The Law of Medical Practice* (1959), 136
Shepard, *The Love Treatment* (1971), 7, 95
Sifneos, "Change in Patient's Motivation for Psychotherapy," 128 *Am. J. Psychiat.* 718 (1971), 17, 24
Stafford-Clark, Book Review, 74 *Yale L.J.* 392 (1964), 2
Sullivan: *The Psychiatric Interview* (1954), 24
Szasz: *Law, Liberty and Psychiatry* (Collier Books 1968), 100, 106, 127
________ *The Myth of Mental Illness* 4 (Delta Book 1961), 2, 17

Taylor, *The Law in its Relation to Physicians* (1900), 86
The Times (London) Nov. 25, 1960, 95
Thompson (Ed.): *An Outline of Psychoanalysis* (1955), 56, 93

Ungerleider, "That Most Difficult Year," 122 *Amer. J. Psychiat.* 542 (1965), 56, 57
Vinogradoff: *Common Sense in Law* (1959), 117

Wall, J.H.: "The Psychiatric Problem of Suicide," 101 *Am. J. Psychiat.* 404 (1944), 133
Watson: *Psychiatry for Lawyers* (1968), xi, 24
Wharton & Stille, *Medical Jurisprudence*, 22
Wheelis, "To Be a God," 36 *Commentary* 125 (1963), 24, 52
Witenberg, Rioch and Mazer: "The Interpersonal and Cultural Approaches," in 2 *Amer. Handbook Psychiat.* 1417 (Arieti ed. 1959), 142

INDEX OF BOOKS, ARTICLES, AND OTHER SOURCES

SUBJECT INDEX